The Manager's Pocket Guide to
Social Media

Richard Brynteson, Ph.D.
Jason DeBoer-Moran, MBA
Carol Zacher Rinkoff, Ph.D.

HRD Press, Inc. v Amherst, MA

Copyright © 2011 by HRD Press, Inc.

> HRD Press, Inc.
> 22 Amherst Road
> Amherst, Massachusetts 01002
> 1-800-822-2801 (U.S. and Canada)
> (413) 253-3488
> (413) 253-3490 (fax)
> http://www.hrdpress.com

No part of the material should be reproduced or utilized in any form or by any means, electronic or mechanical, including photocopying, recording, or by information storage and retrieval systems without written permission from the publisher.

ISBN 978-1-59996-258-0

Production services by Jean S. Miller
Cover design by Eileen Klockars
Editorial services by Sally M. Farnham

DEDICATIONS

Dedicated to my mother, Pat, and Aunt Marion, who have lived fulfilled lives without ever having tweeted.

– Richard

Dedicated to my wife, Erin, for her support as I wander in virtual worlds, and to my daughter, Ellis, who was born as this book was being written.

– Jason

Dedicated to my son Matt and his wife, Amanda, and my son Evan and his wife, Cara. Thanks, kids, for friending me on Facebook. And in my real life, too.

– Carol

Thanks to McKenzie Malanaphy for the fine editing job he did for us.

– Richard, Jason, and Carol

The Manager's Pocket Guide to Social Media
Contents

Chapter 1. The Evolution of Social Media 1

Chapter 2. Why Care? 17

Chapter 3. The Rise of Strategic Authenticity and Transparency... 33

Chapter 4. The Social Psychology of Social Media 45

Chapter 5. Social Media as Communication Management.. 59

Chapter 6. Social Media as a Marketing Tool 69

Chapter 7. Social Media as an Innovation Tool.................. 89

Chapter 8. Creating People Partnerships Using Social Media... 105

Chapter 9. Managing Strategy Using Social Media 117

Chapter 10. Metrics and Social Media 129

Chapter 11. Social Capital: The Deposits and Withdrawals of Social Media 143

Chapter 12. The Ethics of Social Media............................ 159

Chapter 13. The Future of Social Media 173

Final Tweets 179

References and Websites... 181

Chapter 1
The Evolution of Social Media

Prelude

April 1775: Tensions were running high between the British and Colonialists in and around Boston. The Boston Massacre and the Boston Tea Party earlier in the decade had heightened the disagreements. It was rumored that the British were going to march on the Colonial strongholds of Lexington and Concord. Responding to a lantern signal from the Old North Church (one if by land, two if by sea), the rabble rouser, silversmith, and great connector Paul Revere raced from Boston to warn the villagers that the British were coming. At one in the morning, he galloped from village to village, farmhouse to farmhouse, yelling out the warning. By dawn's early light, the Colonialists had assembled more than 70 men to meet the British forces.

During January and February of 2011, Egyptian youth took to the streets of Cairo to protest the corrupt regime of Hosni Mubarak. Although the reasons for the protests were widespread hunger and poverty in the country, social media tools catalyzed and helped the spread of the protests. Two events seemed to spark the successful rebellion. First, the successful neighboring Tunisia rebellion was well publicized. Second, a Facebook page was created (by Google executive Wael Ghonim) protesting the beating death of an Egyptian businessman who had exposed government corruption. Protestors were called together in Tahrir Square, day after day, by Twitter and Facebook users. Demonstrators stayed in communication through these social media tools. Mubarak recognized the power of these tools, tried to thwart them, but was ultimately unsuccessful.

Did social media cause this rebellion? No, activists had been working toward this goal for years. Poverty galvanized Arab youth all over the region. But the social media tools mobilized protestors. Social media magnified the message. Ironically, Facebook and Twitter do exactly what Mubarak did not do for almost three decades: listen and engage.

In both of these uprisings, the rebels used the best available technology to spread the word and mobilize. For Colonialists, social media was a horseman and roads; the Egyptians used Facebook, YouTube, and Twitter. The Colonialists lost the first battle at Lexington, but won the war. Many Egyptian protestors died and were injured in these days of rage, but Mubarak was ultimately toppled.

What Is Social Media?

Social media is a variety of tools, mostly online, that facilitate conversations between people. Social media tools allow participants to share their ideas, beliefs, pictures, videos, files, or promotions with one, a few, or the multitudes. These tools facilitate connections in new places.

The Evolution of Social Media

Social media, sometimes referred to as Web 2.0, is highly portable and easily accessible. People who connect using social media may be friends and family, company and consumer, cause and donor, evangelist and follower, or just all those people who love their pet ferrets deeply. Successful social media is user-generated engagement, where users see and interact with what they have created. Because of this, social media has democratized media: the voices of many, rather than the few, can be heard. Social media expedites conversations rather than pushing content. Social media tools facilitate the building of online communities.

The Principal Forms of Social Media

- **Social Networking Sites:** Facebook, MySpace, Classmates.com. These sites allow users to share and exchange thoughts, events, ideas, articles, and other content. Typically, members have to accept your request to be their "friend."

- **Blogs/Microblogs:** WordPress, Blogspot, Tumblr, Twitter. Users "blog" (write an essay) on any special or general interest subject; anyone can read these blogs. The microblog Twitter allows only 140 characters; these are small messages. Google Plus is the newest innovation in this arena.

- **Location-Based Mobile Platform:** Foursquare, Gowalla, Loopt. These platforms connect users at specific locations, primarily businesses. They encourage participation by offering discounts and information about those businesses.

- **Online Game Worlds:** World of Warcraft, online poker, Farmville. Users play these games in groups or as individuals, and many are very elaborate. Some are even used in curriculum at universities.

- **Open Source Projects:** Wikipedia. These cooperative endeavors allow geographically dispersed populations to collaborate on projects.

- **File-Sharing Communities:** Photobucket, Flickr. These communities come together around common interests and share their files. For instance, Flickr users share photographs and have built a common library of millions of images.

- **Virtual Social Worlds:** Secondlife. In these "worlds," players create a new life for themselves online, sometimes spending and making real money in these fantasy worlds.

Like most tools, social media has upsides and downsides. On the upside, social media can enable productive conversations, connect people for creative collaboration, and bring disparate worlds together to solve problems. Social media can make people into more savvy consumers. Also on the positive, many life-affirming causes have raised millions of dollars in order to help earthquake victims, impoverished people, and endangered species.

Despite its positives, social media can be a huge time-waster, sucking valuable hours from an employee, a student, or a citizen. It can also be an avenue to unhealthy addictions. Many users display narcissism through excessive blogging and picture sharing. Others use social media as a substitute for the real world, engaging with handheld devices rather than real individuals. Car accidents occur from texting and tweeting. Many individuals have checked into expensive rehabilitation centers to break their addictions to online gaming. There is even one reported case of a neglected baby dying of starvation while its parents played online collaborative games.

What Is this Book About?

This is not a how-to book or a book with screen shots. This is not a book about the intricacies of technology nor is it an exhaustive look at all social media sites outside of management implications. We'll leave that to other authors. We are not promoting or shunning any given technology or tool, or any specific use of these tools. Social media will inevitably play a different role in each individual's life.

Instead, we are offering the general manager a solid look at the field of social media. We will outline, in clear and simple English, the ways that social media can be employed as a management tool. The reader can learn how social media can be used as a management, marketing, and communication tool. A manager can see how various companies have improved both their status with social media and also allowed these tools to hurt them. Together we will examine the history and philosophies underpinning these new tools.

This book...

will include...	will not include...
pros and cons of social media brief historical context management applications important questions tips and techniques	screen shots how-to's promotions micro-level confusion exact "rights" or "wrongs" confusing technical jargon

A Brief History of Communication: Crossed Spears and Tin Cans

The tension between the group and the individual has been a constant in organizations and societies. Who has the power, the group or the individual? How and why does communication about group norms happen? Who makes the rules? Who is part of the group and who is not?

Communication—whether between individuals and groups, groups and groups, or individuals and individuals—will always exist using available technology. Native Americans used smoke signals to communicate over miles. Amazonian jungle natives used crossed spears to indicate that nonmembers of the "group" were not allowed to enter a territory. Unfortunately, many westerners did not understand this message and lost their heads (literally) as a result. African tribes often used drums to communicate with each other. Hieroglyphics have been used from Egypt to South America as a communication device from one group to another.

Within groups and tribes, storytelling around the campfire has been a powerful social media. These stories, whether dealing with creation or the exploits of gods or great warriors, passed the fundamentals of a culture from one generation to another, and took hours to tell, not 140 characters.

Roads and rivers also constituted early social media conduits. News was passed up and down rivers in canoes. One thousand years ago, runners would carry messages along the old Inca Road stretching over a thousand miles in the Andes. The Silk Road served a similar purpose in central Asia. Towns in medieval Europe developed at crossroads of major trading routes. Medieval fairs organically sprung up at these crossroads as a way of meeting and greeting, trading, and communing once a year. Several hundred years later, the fur trapper voyageurs of North America came together once a year with their encampments, and a couple weeks of trading, selling, drinking, and merrymaking. At the same time, North American natives gathered together at Powwows for dancing, storytelling, and communion of geographically dispersed tribes. The last large Powwow was held by about 6,000 natives from the tribes of the northern tribes of America along the Bighorn River in July 1876. George Armstrong Custer and his men unsuccessfully crashed that party.

Sometimes individuals are expelled by groups, such as "shunning" in North American Amish culture. This happens when a member breaks group norms; group members are not allowed to communicate with these "shunned" members. Heretics are kicked out of the church. Unruly children are given "time-outs." Today, expulsion can also come in the form of "de-friending" on Facebook, when a person chooses to break cyberspace ties with a member of their online network.

Recent History of Social Media

Social media is a 21st century phenomenon brought about by innovations in technology. The development of internet, email, wireless, file sharing, Global Positioning System (GPS), and mobile communication has accelerated the progress of social media tools and technology.

Previously established mail systems—such as passenger pigeons, the Pony Express, and courier systems—facilitated communication. Thomas Edison's telegraph sent messages across lines from point A to point B. The movable type press allowed for mass printing; the same "Wanted: Dead or Alive" poster could be distributed to thousands of people. Billboards are viewed by thousands on a daily basis. The telephone allows communication over large expanses of space. It should be noted that as recently as World War II the world leaders Churchill and Roosevelt communicated primarily by letter. All these technologies have been partially supplanted by web-based and virtual technologies, but they have also given rise to social media.

Technological social networking is not new to the end of the 20th century. "Phone-phreaking," a phenomenon of the 1950s, involved technological geeks tapping into existing phone systems to create conference calls with their friends. Others hacked into corporate phone systems for their conference calls. In 1979, the first "bulletin board system" was created by hooking up small servers and modems for file sharing. Below is a timeline of social media sites and innovations over the past 20 years.

YEAR	SITE	APPLICATION
1969	Compuserve (later AOL)	First online service; biggest player in the 1980s
1984	Prodigy	First nationwide online system developed in 1990
1988	IRC	The first Internet Relay Chat is invented

Mid 1990s		First individual real online service
1997	Six Degrees	First social networking site allowing connection among friends
1998	*You've Got Mail*	Tom Hanks and Meg Ryan build a relationship using email
1999	Napster	First efficient online file sharing used for sharing music files; deemed illegal a short time later
2000	BoingBoing	Popular lifestyle and culture newsletter moves completely to a blog-based communication tool
2001	Stumbleupon	Internet community where users rate websites
2002–3	Friendster	Popular friend connection site
2003	Flickr and Photobucket	Photo file sharing
2004 or 2006	Digg	Social news website where readers can rate the value of stories
2004	Myspace	Allowed users to customize profile; most popular social networking site 2004–6

The Evolution of Social Media

2004	Facebook	Began as a college only service to connect students
2005	Reddit	Social news website; users can comment and post; purchased by Condé Nast Digital in 2006
2005	YouTube	Popular site for video sharing
2006	Twitter	By the end of the decade, "tweeting" is popularized
2007	The reign of Facebook is established	Takes over as the most popular networking site
2007	Friendfeed (bought by Facebook)	Allows integration of Twitter, Flickr, RSS feeds, Facebook
2008	Delicious	Social bookmarking web service
2009	FourSquare	Location-based social platform
2009	Quora	Question and answer social media site
2010	*The Social Network*	Golden Globe Winner tells the story of the founding of Facebook
2011	Google Plus	Google introduces its seven social media tools

Chapter Summaries

Below is a list of the chapters in this book—this is where we are going.

1. **The Evolution of Social Media:** New delivery service, same old story. This chapter gives a context for the development of social media engagement and an overview of popular social media sites.

2. **Why Care?** Why should we care about social media? Social media facilitates a variety of exchanges: social, emotional, intellectual, and others. These exchanges are the foundations of our society.

3. **The Rise of Strategic Authenticity and Transparency:** Online tools encourage transparency and demand authenticity; these are the new rules.

4. **The Social Psychology of Social Media:** Social psychology deals with how people interact in group settings. This chapter applies the principles of social psychology to social media.

5. **Social Media as Communication Management:** How can social media effectively facilitate communication internally and externally for an organization?

6. **Social Media as a Marketing Tool:** Social media tools constitute a wealth of goods and services.

How can a manager use these tools effectively for selling a product or service?

7. **Social Media as an Innovation Tool:** Social media can be a powerful management tool or a productivity waster. Managers—do not ignore this tool, harness it!

8. **Creating People Partnerships Using Social Media:** Social media facilitates the recruitment, hiring, training, and maintenance of a healthy workforce.

9. **Managing Strategy Using Social Media:** Social media can be a powerful strategy tool for top leadership.

10. **Metrics and Social Media:** Social media is here to stay (at least until the next thing); how do we assess its impact?

11. **Social Capital: The Deposits and Withdrawals of Social Media:** Social media is examined in terms of social capital exchange and the unpredictability of its participants.

12. **The Ethics of Social Media:** Social media is like Janus, the two-headed god of Roman mythology; it can be both good and evil. This chapter explores the ethical issues around social media.

13. **The Future of Social Media:** What is the future of social media?

Final Tweets: How do we put all of this together?

Who Are We?

This book is a collaboration between three unique individuals, each with a different and dynamic relationship with social media.

- **Dr. Richard Brynteson** is a Professor of Management specializing in adult education at Concordia University and an organizational innovation consultant who has authored books on innovation and systems thinking. Richard is curious and fascinated by the way friends flow between the "real" world and "virtual" world and sees social media as playing a big role in the future of education.

- **Jason DeBoer-Moran** is the Assistant Director of Computer User Services for Concordia University in St. Paul, Minnesota, where he teaches a graduate course in strategic communication management and an undergraduate course in electronic marketing. Jason was voted one of the top 20 innovative social media users in Minneapolis/St. Paul, Minnesota, in 2009 by a panel of peers.

- **Dr. Carol Rinkoff** is the Assistant Vice President of Academic Affairs at Argosy University, Twin Cities campus, and has taught both graduate and undergraduate university courses in organizational management. Carol has used social media seriously (for organizational strategy and marketing) and recreationally (playing social media games with online friends around the world).

Chapter 2
Why Care?

The Museum of Science and Industry, Chicago

In 2010, the Museum of Science and Industry in Chicago sponsored a contest (Scott, n.d.). They offered $10,000 to someone willing to live in the museum and blog to the world about his or her experience. The winner was long-time resident of Chicago, 24-year-old Kate McGroarty, who posted daily blogs and YouTube videos. She wrote and talked about the exhibits, the curators, the janitors, the visitors—anything that was interesting. Many people responded to her online logs, posting their reactions and favorite memories of the museum. The museum even created a Facebook page about the 24-year-old's adventures.

Essentially, Kate raised a curtain by allowing followers and participants to experience the inner workings of the museum. The results, measured in new online friends of the museum and prevalence of quality conversations concerning the facility, surpassed the museum's expectations. The museum was able to use social media tools in a novel and engaging event that benefitted its publicity and public engagement.

It's Here, Like it or Not

Social media is here, like it or not. Social media can be sweet and loving or vicious. It becomes a part of the day to day, a part of the changing face of America, just like the computer and the internet. It can build businesses and it can destroy governments. Regardless of its many functions, its presence is powerful. It is embraced by your employees, your boss, your children, and maybe even your grandmother. So, why care? Here's why:

- You want to understand what that whiz kid in marketing is talking about during strategy meetings.
- Knowledge of social media is necessary in order to be conversant with your Millennial-Generation employees (without them rolling their eyes at how "out of the loop" you are).
- You want access to industry information faster than the competition or your boss.
- You want to be able to see pictures of your cute, little grandchildren.
- You want to know what your children are giggling about in their bedrooms.
- You have learned that social media might be the key to building your brand or your organization's brand.

- You want to finally be able to finish Friday's *New York Times* crossword puzzle.
- You want to figure out which cable company's pricing is less deceptive.
- You want to improve your bottom line, your competitive advantage, and your agility for innovation.

We cannot predict what social media will look like ten years from now, but we can guarantee it is not a fad; the need for engagement is here to stay.

Trends Leading to Social Media

Social media is not about new technology; it is the convergence of social, economic, technological, and global forces in the 21st century. As we shall see in this book, many of these forces are undeniable and unstoppable. These forces include but are not limited to:

- The expectation of connectivity in the Millennial Generation: They were born in an era of electronic devices, IMing, texting, and "friending," which are as natural as eating, breathing, and worshipping Hannah Montana or Justin Timberlake. National parks have even begun providing Wi-Fi in order to keep the interest of younger generations. Many young people have never used a phone with a cord.

- Fear and loathing of traditional advertising: Advertising experienced a meteoric rise during the last half of the 20th century. Its excesses and semi-truths have turned off consumers; trust in advertising has diminished severely.
- The embrace of a 24/7 business culture: Checking one's Blackberry at 2:00 a.m. is not uncommon. We are not stating that this trend is healthy, just that it drives communication trends. Social media access is always available, always compelling, and always ready to suck otherwise wasted hours away from the insomniac.
- Technology advances: I'll check my profile in the sky, I'll check my profile under the sea, I'll check my profile in a box, with a fox, with a mouse, in a house, etc. Technology allows us to check emails, texts, news flashes, and blogs during funerals, while flying airplanes off course, during a honeymoon, or while otherwise engaged in crucial conversations. The iPod, Blackberry, iPad, and other mobile device technology have facilitated the popularity and prevalence of social media.
- Physical adeptness: Starting with the use of joysticks and continuing on with the widespread use of cell phones, iPods, Wii, and Xbox Kinect, users have developed new muscles and new finger coordination. Some theorists even claim that we are developing a generation of people with

"monkey thumbs" because of the thumb versatility people are developing. We know that a quarter of our traditional college students can text with their cell phones in their pockets.

- The world feels more complex: With this complexity comes a yearning to be more efficient. Not enough time to create invitations for your graduation party? Just create an event on Facebook or Evite, and the right "friends" will show up.

- The world is shrinking: Students in Istanbul talk to students in Seoul who want to talk to students in Peoria. Dell Computer's software teams co-create from Penang, London, Bangalore, and Austin. Virtual teams tackle global warming issues, save children, bring down criminal syndicates, smuggle opium, and develop religious liturgies. Social media helps connect these teams, for better or for worse.

Why Care? Exchanges Are *Us*

Our lives are made up of exchanges. We exchange oxygen for carbon dioxide, Clif bars for the physical energy to run 10 miles, taxes for protection from evil forces and for the right of our children to attend overpopulated schools with bullies. This notion is the basis of social media. Below are the most common exchanges facilitated by social media sites.

Emotional Exchanges

Twelve-step groups, family reunions, funerals, and two eight-year-olds sharing quietly at the edge of the playground are all involved in emotional exchanges. In the past, emotional exchanges would often occur from front porch to front porch, from tuna casserole to coffee after church. Social media sites have facilitated emotional exchanges between people separated by great distances.

CaringBridge (http://www.caringbridge.org/) is a nonprofit website designed to help those with serious illnesses communicate with their loved ones. In the old days, loved ones of those undergoing surgery or other serious procedures had to call others for updates, or establish phone trees. CaringBridge provides blogs, updates, and notes that allow for constant updates, responses, and shows of support from friends and family. CaringBridge can facilitate a supportive community around the sick person and enhance communication around that person.

Funeral homes have also tapped into social media as an emotional support system. When facing the death of a loved one, friends and family can post remembrances, thoughts, prayers, and wishes to the family of the deceased using a blog-type format. Through these tools, a community is formed around the deceased. Emotional exchanges can occur on Facebook, Twitter, blogs, and other media sites. Here, participants often share and explore their feelings concerning traditionally difficult or touchy issues. The division between private and public communication spaces is sometimes blurred.

Friendship Exchanges

These exchanges are similar to emotional exchanges, but may not be as intense, drama-based, or emotional. SixDegrees, Friendster, Myspace, Bebo, Twitter, Classmates, and Facebook are all tools to find, build, and maintain friends and acquaintances. These sites allow people to connect with others and stay abreast of recent events and other people's lives.

With more than 500 million users in 2010, Facebook was by far the most popular of these sites. Users cite its versatility as a point of interest. One can "friend" or "de-friend" people on Facebook. Status Updates allow friends to read about your day-to-day exploits and interests, view your pictures, and read articles that you have written or that you think are interesting. Many people open their website browsers to the familiar Facebook homepage as the first point of entry. In early 2011, Facebook was valued at $50 billion.

Twitter serves as a different type of message site. Unlike the unfettered message length on Facebook, Twitter is a mini-message site that limits users to 140 characters. Quick messages and status updates relay information to "followers": "Burritos are excellent at Chipotle's today," "Starbuck's has

$1 off lattes from 3-5pm," or "Check out this article on red-wing sapsuckers." As with any social media, Twitter can be a swift conveyor of useful (and potentially life-saving) information, or a time-waster, "I'm bored at work today." In late 2010, Twitter was "valued" at over $3 billion.

Another form of the friendship site is found in dating services like Match.com or eHarmony.com. A member pays a monthly fee for these virtual match-makers and can scan other members' profiles in search of a suitable partner. Believe it or not, current studies suggest that almost 20 percent of recent marriages had their start from online dating sources.

Recreational Exchanges

"Let's play gin rummy in the parlor together" has been supplanted by "Let's plant side-by-side farms together on Farmville," "Will you be my ally on Mafia wars?" or "Will you play on my fantasy football team?" Friends can recreate together on a variety of sites from Facebook to Second Life to World of Warcraft. In the old days, we played Monopoly and Clue together on the living room floor or at the dining room table. Now, we recreate online. Even Solitaire, once a game played by oneself (or with another) with a physical deck of cards, is now played online.

Why Care?

Although some research suggests that we are becoming a nation of strangers who now "bowl alone," other research indicates that these games are bringing us together in camaraderie. Teams collaborate, build strategies, and work together to win. Interaction is a must, a necessity, and in many cases, a joy.

Online games like Second Life, World of Warcraft, and EverQuest, far from being time wasters, can also teach business, leadership, and team-building skills. Because of these benefits, online games are being used by some business schools.

Intellectual Exchanges

A friend, Michael, is an active participant in Goodreads, a social networking site for people who wish to share their favorite book choices. Here, participants befriend others and share their favorite books and discuss them. Another site, bookgasm.com, offers a similar service, but is open-source, meaning that anyone can post a book review. It is also a for-profit—funded by advertisements.

RSS news feeds also qualify as intellectual exchange sites. A person can set up their news feed so that they receive regular updates on subjects that they have pre-selected based on their personal interests. Other social media sites like Facebook and Twitter also allow users to send intellectual tidbits, articles, or ideas to friends and followers.

Quora is a recent intellectual exchange site. The power of this website is the ability to ask questions to be answered by experts. A person can pose a question, say about the Bataan Death March and it might be forwarded to a survivor of that march.

Material Exchanges

A capitalistic economy is, first and foremost, about material exchange. Previously, these exchanges happened at town fairs, at village markets, and in stores, and they still do. They also occur in some communities with barter systems where people pool their services such as babysitting, plumbing, housework, web design, and lawyering. By performing services, they receive credits that can be traded for other services that they need.

Craigslist and eBay take the lead in material exchanges online. Craigslist is an extensive bartering, connecting, hiring, and selling social networking site where one can buy bikes, rent condos, find a job, claim free stuff, and find a suitable (or unsuitable) partner. Craigslist eliminates the middleman from the quest to find and buy the right boat, book, or hooker for the right price. Plus, kiss taxes goodbye. On the other hand, Craigslist has been responsible for connections that have led to fraud and murder.

On the popular auction site eBay, people can auction off family diamond brooches, tickets to popular concerts, and record collections. Money is passed through PayPal, a secure and free site that facilitates the transfer of money.

Professional Exchanges

Job seekers no longer wait with bated breath for the Sunday newspaper and the want ads. Instead, they click on Monster.com and other such sites to search online. These job matchmaking sites allow users to post their resumes (or even podcasts) and peruse job openings all around the world.

A prominent professional exchange site is LinkedIn, an occupation-oriented social media site. With LinkedIn, each user creates a professional profile and views the profiles of others. One can acquire references and recommendations from colleagues and post them for potential employers to read. LinkedIn profiles are fast taking the place of resumes as initial screenings made by human resource departments for job searches.

Consumer Exchanges

Customers use social media sites to express pleasure and dissatisfaction with companies on social media sites. YouTube videos documented a service representative falling asleep on a couch and a guitar being broken by a major airline. Flickr photos show pot holes, poorly done delivered food, and malfunctioning digital signage.

Political Exchanges

Social media sites have become the playground for politicians. These sites were used extensively by President Obama for raising money and garnering support from younger members of the populous. Harnessing the reach and sway of social media is quickly becoming a mainstay of political fundraising and campaigning. Engaging in social media, at least Facebook and Twitter, is a necessary element of modern politics. And, as we read in Chapter 1, social media sites are used by political subgroups for communicating and creating joint action.

Crisis Exchanges

Twitter and texting are moving important messages faster than any other media. In 2009, a student at Virginia Tech tragically shot and killed over 30 fellow students. In the wake of that incident, campuses began collecting Twitter accounts and cell phone numbers from students to warn them of disasters and moments of crisis. A Twitter account, with dozens or hundreds of "followers," can pass important and potentially life-saving news very quickly.

Another example of the use of social media sites during a crisis emerged from the tragic Haitian earthquake in January 2010, where over 200,000 people were killed. Following the disaster, social media sites opened by NGOs (nongovernmental organizations) raised money for the survivors and helped loved ones reconnect.

Aesthetic Exchanges

If murderers, thieves, and do-good fundraisers can use social media sites, why not aesthetically minded art lovers? They do. Just check out Flickr, a very popular photography site to see the extent of the art world's participation online. Amateur and professional photographers have accumulated over 3.5 million photos on this site for anyone to view and use. Took a trip to Europe? Store your photos in a file on Flickr and share them with your relatives and friends. Had your first child? Create a file for the 1,485 incredibly special and totally cute pictures of her so that they can be shared with grandparents, uncles, and cousins who are all waiting expectantly to view the future president of the United States.

Personal Branding: The Great Leveling

It started with Fred Rogers. Every day at 4:00 p.m. for two decades, Mr. Rogers, the TV personality, told millions of children, "You are so special." As these children grew, they played on soccer teams where everyone received a trophy and a gold ribbon whether or not they touched the ball or their team even played a real game. These children were carted around from piano lessons to ballet to whiffle ball in minivans and handed a quality life by their doting parents. Why shouldn't they have their own brand, blog, and Facebook identity?

Whether you like it or not, you have always had a brand. Five centuries ago, you may have been the village idiot, the grumpy old recluse, or the town crier (a busy-body spreading news from one source to another). Even Grog, our ancestor living in a cave, might have been branded by his tribe as "deer killer" or "stew cooker."

In those days, your brand may have been limited to a few-mile radius. Some had more widespread brands. Genghis Khan, Alexander the Great, Jesus, Buddha, and Blackbeard the Pirate had broader brands. With the internet and social media, brands have become widespread. Lady Gaga, Bono, LeBron James, Tiger Woods, and Osama Bin Laden all have worldwide brands founded on their actions, public relations, and social media. For better or worse, globalism, Web 2.0, and the media have all impacted the spread of the fortunes and misfortunes of personal brands.

But again, "why care?" **You have a personal brand, whether you like it or not.** What is that brand going to be? Reputations, or brands, are made, borrowed, stolen, stumbled upon, or backed into. Google and other forces have a part in the creation of your brand. But you have a bigger part. Are you a passive or an active force in creating how the world sees you? Are you consciously or unconsciously branding yourself?

Why Care?

Unfortunately, many people (young people in particular) do not realize that they are creating an image, persona, or brand through their social media usage. Erin, 17, does not realize that her negative postings set a tone for how people regard her. Jason, 19, does not understand that the slurs and swear words he uses on Facebook impact how future colleges or employers view him. Sixteen-year-old Brittany's ramblings about her recent breakup with her boyfriend are available for the world to see.

When questioned, several colleagues of ours admitted that they have rejected applicants because of profanity in their Facebook accounts. A church-related employer admitted to firing an employee for the sexual content of his Facebook profile, and a big box retailer recently let an employee go because of their derogatory comments on an "I hate ____ (retailer)" site. All of these examples demonstrate how social media users often fail to realize the full impact of their online comments and posts.

Questions you may wish to ask yourself include:

- How am I showing up in the world? What is my current brand?

- Who does Google say that I am? (Go ahead, Google yourself!)

- In what ways can I enhance my brand, image, or public persona?

- How am I inadvertently detracting from my image?
- What social media tools might be best for me to use, given my personal brand goals?

Chapter 3
The Rise of Strategic Authenticity and Transparency

Punch Pizza

Punch Pizza is a Neapolitan pizza shop with seven locations in the Minneapolis and St. Paul metro area. They offer an authentic wood-fired Neapolitan pizza experience, and their passion for this authenticity is so strong that they have gone to great lengths to maintain it. In order to ensure authenticity, their pizza chefs are certified by the Vera Pizza Napoletana, the "pizza police" of Napoli, Italy. The unique pizza oven used to create their pizza is located right at the front of the store. Customers can watch as their pizza roasts at 800 degrees for 90 seconds. This experience is the differentiator that separates Punch Pizza from other pizza chains.

When Punch Pizza first opened, they had a strict no photography policy. They did not want the design of their ovens or the techniques that their certified chefs use to leak out to the competition. Because it takes five years to train a chef, Punch invests a significant amount of time and money in the certification process. The owner reasoned that photos and videos could jeopardize their investment because they could lose their competitive edge in the high margin restaurant market. This policy began to cost Punch some notoriety in the local community as several well-known food bloggers were informed they were not allowed to take photos of the restaurant.

A Twin Cities pizza blogger, Aaron Landry, was attempting to document his experience at Punch and was informed that he was not permitted to photograph the oven. He blogged about his experience, and several other photographers and local food personalities shared their mutual frustration with the policy. Unknowingly, Punch had alienated some of their most passionate fans (Landry, 2007).

Punch began the processes of establishing an online presence only to realize that a presence had already been created for them. People who were passionate about their restaurant had launched a Facebook fan page; Flickr was full of contraband photos of their restaurant. The owners could have filed a cease and desist order or petitioned to shut down this content but instead harnessed this passion to build their brand. They removed their restrictive photography policy and encouraged photography with a "Capture Our Fire" contest. Anyone who submitted a photo of their Punch experience was entered in a contest to win gift cards. They were strategically transparent. They were willing to disclose some of their business secrets to increase the passion of their fans. The public responded by shooting photos that were then licensed for use on their website.

The Rise of Strategic Authenticity and Transparency

Social media has empowered customers and employees to share their experiences with the world. Before social media, companies could easily dictate which information was for public consumption versus internal use. Companies shared success stories through press releases and scandal broke through formal reporting and investigation. These tools are now in the hands of countless civilian reporters—customers and employees. CNN has even created iReport, an outlet for civilian reporters to submit videos and stories for consideration in their formal newscast. Customers are skeptical of businesses that live in secrecy. Companies are now faced with the question, "What are we comfortable with sharing?"

Definitions of Transparency

The tools that power social media are based on the premise of exchanges. It is possible that as customers and employees exchange knowledge through social media, they purposefully or inadvertently draw attention to the things that managers hoped would remain undisclosed. The act of exchanging illuminates areas by shining light into the dark. Facebook cofounder Mark Zuckerberg summarizes the power of social media, saying, "By giving people the power to share, we're making the world more transparent" (Baumann, 2011, para. 1). Social media has become the light that shines through your organization for both good and bad. It is advisable not to ignore this power.

The counterpart to transparency is authenticity. When corporate representatives begin to communicate through social media, it is essential that they communicate authentically. A failure to be perceived as authentic is often more detrimental than a lack of involvement with social media. In order to be authentic, corporate representatives must be seen throughout the community as trustworthy and genuine. The community must recognize them as the corporate voice, and this voice must appear to be controlled by a real person and not completely governed by corporate authority. If you position a customer service representative as one of the voices of your corporation, that individual must hear complaints and act when complaints are actionable. In pursuit of authenticity, this representative cannot simply read a script or repeat a corporate message; he or she must be an individual with a personality, passion, and a deep understanding of your organization.

All of your corporate social media users are heard as the voice of your organization, regardless of the legal disclaimers stated in their profiles. Lance Secretan, a leadership coach, speaks to the power of authenticity when considered in the social media context. He explains, "Authenticity is the alignment of head, mouth, heart, and feet—thinking, saying, feeling, and doing the same thing—

consistently. This builds trust, and followers love leaders they can trust" (The Secretan Center, n.d., para. 2). The individuals you commission and encourage to be a part of your legitimate corporate voice will gain followers who are trusting and serve as brand advocates.

Authenticity and transparency cannot be separate endeavors; they inherently intertwine. They continuously ebb, flow, and build upon each other. Secretan's statement about authenticity addresses the relationship between authenticity and an organization that is willing to be strategically transparent. In order to show alignment in thinking, saying, feeling, and acting, you must be willing to disclose and share details. Ultimately, businesses must determine what is shareable and what is not. Punch Pizza disclosed the images of their oven and cooking processes. However, they did not release their recipes or ingredient lists. They engaged their critics, learned from them, and became transparent in an effort to demonstrate their willingness to pursue authenticity.

Increasing Transparency (Marqui, 2010)

- Own organizational mistakes and work to correct them.
- Be clear about who is posting to your corporate accounts.

- Acknowledge and respond to legitimate customer questions and complaints.
- Listen to your customers and ask for suggestions when concerns arise.

Increasing Authenticity (Marqui, 2010)

- Be yourself, identify the voice of your organization, and communicate with it.
- Apologize when appropriate and be earnest in your apologies.
- Learn who your advocates are and interact with them.
- Seek organizational alignment.
- Be sure that everyone internally knows what your company stands for.

Practical Organizational Implications

Following a path of authenticity and transparency has some practical implications for your organization. Regardless of an organization's desire to be active in social media, employees and customers are already active and creating transparency. It is the job of the organization to temper that transparency with authenticity. Organizations assume risk when employees take to social media. Melissa Cefkin, an ethnographer and researcher at IBM, draws attention to these risks. Cefkin explains that concern can result from employees on social media "grumbling about the new project they are on," "sharing IP," or sharing online "in advance of the market, creating a potentially bad reputation for something that's about to launch" (Wladawsky-Berger, 2009, para. 37).

One of the largest implications of the rise of social media is an organization's loss of control over their message. Motrin, for example, created an ad campaign targeting moms who use body sling baby carriers for their infants, creating the possibility for potential back pain. Enough moms felt the ads were demeaning and insulting to create a groundswell of Twitter and social media conversation, resulting in Motrin removing their ad. Charlene Li, coauthor of *Groundswell: Winning in a World Transformed by Social Technologies* (2008) and former Forrester analyst, reminds organizations that in order to be successful with social media it is essential to "realize that you will have to give up the fallacy that you have control" (Davis, 2008, para. 32).

Truth in Branding

As we become aware that we have lost control, it is important to hold fast to the fact that the one thing we can control is how our organizations react when social media unearths problems and makes the organization transparent. In 2011, Taco Bell encountered this exact situation. By creating a positive message and rewarding brand advocates, the company was able to handle an initially negative social media reaction and avoid a potential disaster.

The restaurant chain's trouble arose when it became the target of a class action lawsuit for false advertising. Instead of using actual beef, the lawsuit claimed that Taco Bell used taco meat filling, which mainly consisted of extenders and other non-meat substances such as isolated oat product. The complaint claimed that the majority of the filling consisted of substances other than beef, and that Taco Bell was required to refer to it as taco meat filling, but failed to do so (Morrison, 2011). In reaction to this accusation, Taco Bell embraced Facebook, YouTube, and Twitter. It also took out a full-page ad in several national newspapers, thanking the plaintiffs for the lawsuit. The statements that followed the thank you specifically sought to clarify the products they sold as being 88% beef and 12% secret recipe.

The second arm of the company's counter messaging extended through Facebook. At the time of the lawsuit, Taco Bell had 5.4 million Facebook "likes." They used their Facebook page to give away 10 million free beef tacos to Facebook "likers" who downloaded and printed a coupon. After announcing the campaign, they picked up around 100,000 additional "likes." Taco Bell's CEO, Greg Creed, commented on the Facebook campaign in a prepared statement, saying, "Throughout the beef class action lawsuit, the response and enthusiasm from our Facebook community has [sic] been overwhelmingly positive. We found it only fitting to reward these 5.4 million fans and a friend with a free taco. It's our way of saying thanks for their loyalty and support" (Heine, 2011, para. 5).

Customer Service

One of the timeless examples of customers leveraging social media to create transparency is Dave Carroll's "United Breaks Guitars" trilogy. One day, the passengers on a United flight, along with Dave Carroll and his band, witnessed the flight crew throwing guitars as they unloaded luggage. Carroll attempted to bring this to the attention of various flight attendants—only to be ignored. After landing, Carroll found his $3500 Taylor guitar damaged. After many calls to United and being transferred through multiple customer service channels, Carroll was informed by United that it would do nothing. Carroll felt as though he had been placed in a system designed to frustrate and abandon customers without recourse. He promised the final customer service representative that he would respond to United through video songs and invite his fans to vote for them. His goal was one million hits in one year. Within a week, Dave Carroll's original song "United Breaks Guitars" was featured on CNN, the *LA Times, Chicago Tribune*, *Rolling Stone Magazine,* and the BBC. Apart from being a singer songwriter, Dave Carroll is now running Right Side of Right, an organization established to help customers share their own experiences of being on the right side of a battle with corporate customer service.

Four days after Dave Carroll launched his first video, United Airlines' stock price plunged 10 percent, costing shareholders $180 million, or 51,000 broken Taylor guitars. This tune rallied the customer service complaints that many had with United Airlines. Hearing a common voice and seeing the light shining through a frustrating situation created a movement of unified complainers against United.

Successful Transparency in Leadership

To develop an authentic organization, it is essential for leadership to be transparent and authentic. Organizations that have embraced social media have placed their leadership front and center in social media interactions. The online shoe retailer Zappos is a perfect example of the way that leadership's willingness to be transparent can transcend the corporate structure and allow customers to develop a personal relationship with an employee and a brand. Zappos CEO, Tony Hsieh, is constantly present on Twitter, and his early interactions were not brand related. He actively sought out connections with people who shared his interests. As he followed people, they followed him and built real connections. His updates occasionally featured highlights of life as the CEO of Zappos, but he primarily featured contents from the events he attended, his travels, and articles he was reading.

Hsieh's honest sharing caused customers to connect with him and believe in the Zappos brand. As he continued to interact online, he encouraged similar openness in interactions from staff members throughout the company. The company embraced this transparency so much that it even features tweets as they happen on its corporate web page (http://twitter.zappos.com). While many organizations would consider this intimacy a risk, Hsieh and his team considered it an exercise in honesty and transparency. Zappos continues this culture of transparency by inviting the world to their yearly all-hands meeting and offering free tours of their Las Vegas–based headquarters. They will even pick you up from the airport. By making himself accessible, Hsieh is also making his entire organization accessible. Leadership must be willing to take the plunge in order to encourage the rest of the organization to be truly authentic and transparent.

Future of Transparency and Authenticity

As the use of social media continues to grow and gain accessibility, transparency and authenticity will become even more crucial for organizational success. Companies must prepare to answer difficult questions and engage in challenging conversations with customers, employees, and board members. It will become essential for organizations to identify the communities where their authenticity resonates best and seek out open and honest critique, both positive and negative. These communities will open avenues for new markets and advocates who encourage and defend the brand. Customers will expect an authentic interaction and will want to become close friends with the brand—to develop a relationship. Many of these relationships are established long before the customer even decides to purchase from the company. A failure to connect with today's social-media-powered consumer could result in less support and lower sales in the future.

Chapter 4
The Social Psychology of Social Media

Flash Dances

On November 13, 2010, members of a chorus, dressed as civilians, were waiting in a mall food court. Music from Handel's *Messiah* Hallelujah chorus suddenly rang out. Members of the choir "spontaneously" began singing, treating the food court clients to a beautiful rendition. The bystanders were awed and inspired by the performance. Within a month, over 150,000 people had viewed a YouTube video of the event.

A similar performance of the "Do-Re-Mi" song from *The Sound of Music* was held, with dancing, at the Amsterdam Train Station. Michael Jackson's *Thriller* was sung and danced in Liverpool suddenly by a cast of dozens. These performances, called "flash dances," although seemingly at random, are rehearsed and orchestrated. Judging by the expressions on the onlookers' faces, these dances and concerts delight and amuse. And, with hundreds of thousands of YouTube viewers, they have uplifted, inspired, and entertained a multitude of others.

Social Psychology

Social psychology is defined as the relationship between groups and people. Social psychology concerns group behavior, social influence, interpersonal relations, self and social identity, social perception, and attitude change. Many important and insightful social psychology experiments have yielded interesting insights:

- In the "Stanford Prison Experiment," psychology graduate students were divided into "prisoners" and "guards" and placed in a prison simulation. What happened next, no one could have predicted. People became immersed in their roles as if they were real. Guards began to abuse the prisoners; traumatized prisoners began showing ill effects from their incarceration. The experiment ended early. The lesson learned from this experiment was that normal people will subconsciously conform to their organizational context.

- In another experiment, subjects were ordered to give what they believed to be real "electric shocks" to others. As the subjects turned a knob, the victims in another room pretended to be in pain and screamed out. The subjects were ordered to keep turning up the imaginary shocks, and they did as they were told. The real results of this experiment concerned the way the subjects obeyed their authority figures, despite the intense pain they were causing the victims.

This study revealed that people will obey authority figures before examining their own consciences.

- Seminary students were asked to hastily prepare a sermon on the "Parable of thc Good Samaritan" and career options in the ministry. On their way to deliver these sermons, the seminarians passed a coughing homeless man (actor) crouched on the sidewalk. More than half of the students passed the man without stopping to help. Despite the nature of their studies, their goal orientation (successfully delivering their sermon) superseded the act of true pastoral compassion.

- Groups of students were asked to watch a video of two basketball teams passing a ball as they wove amongst each other. They were asked to count the number of passes. In the middle of the video a person in a gorilla outfit walked onto the court. The majority of the students completely failed to see the gorilla. Goal focus creates perceptual blindness.

- Researchers performed an experiment on New York City's busy 42nd Street. A man stood on the street and intently stared up into the sky. Pretty soon others began looking up, even though there was nothing to be seen.

Examining these social psychology experiments offers significant insights concerning human behavior.

Human behavior influences social media. Social media tools influence the social psychology of humans. Many of Facebook's 500 million users have changed the way they interact with friends as the result of Facebook. Job searches are conducted differently as a result of LinkedIn and Monster.com. Twitter promotes spontaneous connections. Power, influence, and behavior patterns all change as a result of social media. The more followers of a person's blog, the more power that author has in the eyes of prospective publishers. Similarly, online popularity can give a television personality more leverage during contract negotiations.

Different social media channels give people and organizations more influence. Both Seth Godin's and Chris Brogan's blogs and Twitter accounts give them widespread influence among followers. When a mobile taco stand in Los Angeles announces its lunchtime location, many change their lunchtime plans. Spontaneous social media sites brought millions of dollars of aid money to Haiti after its tragic earthquake. Social media tools spread information quickly, sometimes prompting fast action.

Because social media is still in its infancy, significant social psychology experimentation in its sphere has not yet occurred. Thus, we are left with more questions than answers.

- Does use of social media diminish face-to-face social skills?

- Are relationships more superficial because of social media tools?
- How does blog reading affect the reading of printed material?
- Could social media be hurting a country's Gross National Product because it constitutes a significant source of time wasting?
- Is employee productivity impacted by the distractions of social media sites?
- Is the quality of writing deteriorating because of the popularity of abbreviation in social media?

This chapter does not hold the answers to these questions, but it does raise a few important questions.

Social Validation and Social Influence

Social validation is about how we seek approval through others. Social influence is about our influence over others. Social media tools have changed even the way we talk about social influence and social validation.

- "I have 545 friends."
- "243 people are following me on Twitter."
- "I follow Oprah."
- "656 subscribe to my blog, but I get about 834 hits a day."
- "I'm going to de-friend you!"

What do these remarks mean? Simply put, we now have different ways of connecting. A teen might brag about having 458 friends, but many of those "friends" are one-time encounters with people she met at a high school football game. Another teen has a blog whose only followers are her four "BFFs" (best friends forever). In a hurried day, many twitterers skim their tweets, many of which are just sales promotions. People often scan their Facebook—unless they are in math class—then it is an in-depth analysis!

On the other hand, if an influential person (Chris Brogan, Seth Godin, LeBron James, or Lady Gaga) talks up a product through social media, he or she lends credibility to that product, and sales probably rise. For example, the rapper 50 Cent pushed a penny stock and sent its value soaring due to his 3.8 million Twitter followers. Social science research tells us that potential consumers seek *assurance* that their choices are good ones. Oprah thinks it, therefore it is. This is similar to advertisers who purport that "four of five doctors recommend…." Likewise, if I follow Oprah, I am special by association; I feel connected to Oprah—like a sort of friend. In this way, social media provides a new kind of approval and assurance. By extension, this phenomenon can work for companies also.

These new definitions call into question old forms of connection. Much research (concerning primitive tribes, factories, churches, social groups) suggests that 150 is the maximum number of people with which one can be closely connected. Beyond this number, it is difficult to keep track and stay connected. Recent research suggests that we can only be tightly connected to 50 people at the most. What about these Facebook, Twitter, LinkedIn, and blog friends? Most likely, they are just acquaintances. Some theorists call social media friends "weak" connections rather than "strong" connections. Others refute this. Nevertheless, a person's sphere of influence has grown with the spread of social media.

Regardless of the number of friends or followers, the power of the group remains primary. People want to be a part of a group, or something bigger than themselves. People want to be associated with causes they believe in, whether it is defeating breast cancer, helping women in developing countries, or promoting green technology. Furthermore, they want to be affiliated with like-minded individuals who love the Oakland Raiders, crave Starbucks, or worship Bono just as much as they do. If you manage for Target, the Gap, or T.G.I. Friday's, you want as many people as possible to "like" and "follow" your company. People like to define their affiliations, why not have them affiliate with your business?

Social Psychology Concepts

If social media does not have influence, why have countries like China blocked Facebook? Some governments see Facebook as a threat; others see it as an advertising goldmine, a way to connect with populations, connect employer and employee, push new ideas, and collect followers. What do we know about social influence as it relates to social media? Below is a list of social influence concepts and an explanation of how they impact social media.

- **Limit Choices:** People do not like too many choices. When a person makes a major purchase, he or she usually narrows down the options to two, three, or four. Research suggests that having too many options can limit happiness. Thus, if you are making commercial offers through social media, limit the choices. Offer $1 off a medium mocha rather than $1.25 off any latte, $1.50 off a double shot caramel macchiato, and so on.

- **Familiarity:** Familiarity fosters likeability. The more they see you, the more they like you. So, for businesses, the more avenues you run in—Facebook, Twitter, blogs—the more comfortable customers feel with your brand, product, and service—and the more they will hopefully buy from you.

- **Recency/Primacy:** People usually pay attention to the first and last items on a list. Perhaps this is why expert bloggers post early in the morning. This is why you do not want to be in the middle of a pack of emails, offers, tweets, etc.

- **Attraction:** People will most usually buy from and listen to people they find attractive. To many, celebrities such as Oprah and Brad Pitt are extremely attractive as role models. If they tweet, blog, or "like" a product or service, others may buy that item without doing any comparison. Witness the success of Oprah's book club. If you make it onto this list, you'll automatically sell 100,000 copies.

- **Consistency:** Whatever your marketing mix, it has to be internally consistent. People become confused if one source (radio commercial) is saying one thing while a different source (Facebook) is saying another. Confused messages hurt your bond with the customer.

- **Illusion of Scarcity:** Scarcity makes items attractive. Note how Groupon and other coupon companies provide the illusion of scarcity for the products/services they are pushing. They have a clock that counts down the minutes until an offer expires, or they post a warning that there are "only 500 available."

- **Useful Tools:** If a tool is useful, people will use it. Previously, "experts" predicted that Facebook would be a tool for young people. Wrong! Even seniors have embraced it. Why? Because it is the best (and often only) way to see pictures of their grandchildren. Wait until budget-minded seniors latch on to Groupon!

- **Danger: Sex and Food Grab Immediate Attention:** If you're hoping to get noticed online, these content topics are sure to do the trick—just remember to use them judiciously and in the appropriate context.

- **Word of Mouth:** Word of mouth has always been and will continue to be the best advertising mode available. News coming from a friend incites action. This works for nonprofits as well as for-profits. If I tweet a message to 123 of my followers and they re-tweet to an average of 148 followers, then suddenly thousands of people are aware of the necessity of sponsoring a Heifer for a family in Bolivia this Christmas or saving five dollars on a vegan pizza with double tofu.

What is the point? To be effective, social media users need to understand the basics of social psychology and how they apply to social media. If a person mindlessly tweets, they will most likely miss the gorilla stealing their latte or the pedestrian in the crosswalk. Conversely, Madonna deciding she likes your line of underwear can result in millions of others deciding that they do as well.

Reward Theory

Reward theory is simple: reward the behavior you want repeated and punish the behavior you do not. Loyalty programs such as "frequent flier miles" and "buy one, get one" are built upon this concept. The more you buy from us, the more you get for free. Brain research suggests that the emotional midbrain is aroused when a person sees a great deal. He or she is engaged with you!

One great social media example of this phenomenon is T.G.I. Friday's "Fan Woody" campaign. T.G.I. Friday's launched a huge Facebook offer based on a "friendly bet" with a hypothetical fan named Woody. If Woody could get 500,000 Facebook fans by September 30th, 2009, those first 500,000 fans would be entitled to a free Jack Daniel's Burger or Chicken Sandwich. T.G.I. Friday's posted YouTube videos and updates from Woody. Using this campaign, the restaurant chain collected tens of thousands of "fans" and boatloads of publicity.

The use of reward theory can also be more subtle. Companies try to coerce visitors to a website to make a small commitment to their enterprise. Visitors can earn rewards for clicking on ads, signing up for special offers, and pressing the "like" button so that their 545 friends see that they love Buffalo

Burger Bob's in East Armpit, South Dakota. Get the viewer to say that they "like" us, and then they might buy from us. Get them to spend more time on our website, and they will be more likely to make a purchase. Buy an iPod today, "fall in love" with the product, and maybe you will buy a MacBook next year.

A subset of reward theory is the arena of reciprocity. People reciprocate gifts. This is not new; remember when that nonprofit sent you a small gift, like return stickers for envelopes and you felt like donating? Giving a little something to your target market breeds an attitude of reciprocity.

Changing Attitudes and Storytelling

Stories change behaviors. Some of the greatest leaders of all time, including Jesus and Confucius, used stories to paint a picture that their followers could understand. Stories told by authority figures, attractive people, or strong connectors are even more impactful. Fundraisers for the Haitian victims of a recent earthquake told stories of individual survivors. The website Kiva, which connects loaners (from developed countries) and borrowers (from developing countries), has its website sprinkled with stories of people who have used loans to build small businesses.

Which stories are the most impactful? Stories from the heart and those that touch the heart are most impactful. These emotional narratives must be compelling. They are effective if they help individuals act or, as social psychologists say, if they increase "personal agency." They are even more powerful when they are accompanied by pictures. Pictures in and of themselves often tell stories. Stories create individual change—whether that means changing toothpaste brands, donating to war victims, or volunteering at a food shelf.

Conclusion

Users of social media would be remiss not to study the concepts of social psychology when engaging audiences. We know much about how people and groups of people work, communicate, and respond to each other. We know that stories of suffering people will prompt some people to open their wallets. We know that some people will not see a gorilla crossing the road when they are texting. We know that some people will follow certain attractive people to the ends of the earth. We know that social media will spread news faster than any previous media. And we know that an organization cannot keep the lid on unattractive stories for very long.

But social media is also changing the rules of social psychology faster and posing more questions than answering them. Is social media creating an addiction response among the young? What would happen if Facebook and Twitter went down for a week? Would we have thousands of nutsy people running around craving connection? Or would we have more presence and serenity in our relationships? If social media can facilitate revolutions and fund raising for excellent causes, what else could these vehicles accomplish? Could social media help cut energy consumption or increase understanding between Christians and Muslims in big ways? Could it help organizations garner resources from unknown sources or hire the perfect employee that they would not have been connected to previously? Could it further the exchange of goods from people to people so unwanted clothes, appliances, and other things would not enter the waste stream?

Chapter 5
Social Media as Communication Management

Social media is often considered only as a marketing tool. However, limiting social media to your marketing department will stifle its power as a communication management tool. Within many organizations, access to mass email lists and full company communication tools is difficult. Internal communication is often heavily guarded, and when too much information is distributed, people tune it out. Social media provides an avenue for those who are interested to explore content that they feel is relevant, and all at a time when they find it convenient. This works not only for external communication, but also for internal communication.

Internal communication challenges are complicated by the rise of young employees. Research suggests that young employees have an aversion to email. A 2006 article in the Chronicle of Higher Education titled "Email Is for Old People" describes the perspective of many recent college graduates in regards to checking email. There is a strong desire for instant, relevant, and personalized communication. As of late, email has become a catch-all tool for blanketed communication that isn't considered relevant, and by the time a millennial actually checks their account, it may no longer be timely. Social media creates an instant, relevant, and personalized platform to speak with these individuals.

External Communication Tools

Tools like Twitter and blogging platforms create a great strength in the economy of characters. Messages must be succinct and to the point in order to be successful. As a result, interested people have a greater tendency to subscribe or follow messages via micro-blogging tools. A tweet of irrelevant communication is more tolerable than a five paragraph email full of pictures and attachments. No one is suggesting that you scrap your email newsletters, but it would be wise to supplement them with a micro-blogging tool like Twitter. One of the greatest powers of social media is the ability to very easily share content. If someone reads an interesting note, they can re-blog or re-tweet it to their community. Messages and news can take on a viral form. They spread, evolve, are commented on, and are made even more relevant through a community's response. Consider the last press release that was distributed by your department or business. How far did it travel? How did you measure how far it traveled? How much further could it have traveled through a social network instead of a standard press release?

PitchEngine is a next generation press release tool powered by social media sites. The company's objective is to help newsmakers "get the word out" to interested media outlets and bloggers. The founder describes PitchEngine as a social PR platform. While standard press release tools and wire services limit the writer to text, PitchEngine integrates with popular social media sites for content and allows the inclusion of attachments. The final press releases are like digital flyers—full of dynamic content that speaks to the new generation of content creators. Clicking "publish" on a pitch distributes it to various social media sites and email accounts. All the major search engines index the news you are sharing, so pitches can be accessed by individuals outside of your sphere of influence.

The Minnesota Department of Transportation uses Twitter (http://twitter.com/mndottraffic) as a reliable communication tool regarding accidents and highway construction. As you can imagine, upper-Midwest roads are often quite dangerous during blizzards. News media can only report so many accidents at one time, and those seeking information often have to wait for it to appear. The Department of Transportation uses Twitter to report new accidents by location. These tweets are only active as long as the lanes are blocked or the road is closed. Once the accident is cleared, the tweets are removed. This allows an interested public to see how bad the roads are before they travel. Because Twitter is built for mobile devices, you can easily visit the site ahead of time and adjust your route appropriately (http://www.startribune.com/local/ 53049377.html).

Social media tools can be used to recruit top talent in a market saturated with opportunities. As employees are increasingly mobile and become more selective about whom they will work for, it becomes necessary for businesses to utilize innovative recruiting efforts that suggest that working for them is different or better. Organizations have begun to create intentionally unpolished YouTube videos to communicate life within the company, because a slick marketing video may cause people to think it is fake or deceptive. Deloitte took a risk and created the Deloitte Film Fest in order to interest new talent (http://www.youtube.com/user/DeloitteFilmFest). The company wanted to capture the experience of being an employee, so it established a contest where current employees could create a short film that answered the question, "What's your Deloitte?" These videos were posted internally and voted on by employees. Deloitte posted the winning videos on YouTube, in addition to using them as part of their recruitment material (Smith, 2008).

Internal Communication Tools

While social media has a reputation for being a tool to facilitate external communication, one should not ignore the power of social media as an internal communication tool. As much as your organization seeks to communicate with the external world, there are internal customers who can benefit from greater connectivity. Sound internal communication creates satisfied employees.

Employees who feel a greater sense of connection within an organization are driven to perform better, generate innovative ideas, and demonstrate a deeper understanding of business objectives and strategic goals. Social media has been leveraged by many in management positions to increase connections between employees across vertical and horizontal reporting structures. "It's easy to keep morale high when the business is doing well, but when things could be better, consistent internal communications buoys morale because employees feel connected," notes Carol Wallace, Director of Marketing Communications at Siemens Business Services, Inc. (META Group, 2004, para. 7).

Social media can be an innovative tool for knowledge capture. Best Buy, a current industry leader in the consumer electronics market, uses an internal social network to harness ideas from its lowest level of employees and deliver them to top strategy implementers across the organization. In contrast, disconnection between higher level management and the hourly employees at Circuit City led in part to its failure. Circuit City originally focused on hiring quality employees who had a great deal of knowledge about the high-end technology it was selling. The corporate office was disconnected from these employees. It rarely asked for input or sought ideas from its key customer-centered staff. Allowing expert staff to interact directly with the customer caused the great success of Circuit City in the 1980s and 1990s. As the economy began to slump, and without a robust internal social network, it was decided that the store would no longer pay the premium price for expert staff. It released some of its most talented employees and replaced them with younger, less-informed staff. The quality of service dropped, and Circuit City closed stores (Mehrmann, 2011).

Best Buy witnessed this downfall and realized that there were two very obvious problems that led to the downfall of Circuit City (Haugen, 2009). First, Circuit City was disconnected from its key customer-facing sales staff. Second, it did not seek to retain the most knowledgeable employees. Thus the Blue Shirt Nation was born. In 2006, the creative director for Best Buy Corporate, Gary Koelling, and Steve Bendt, an account supervisor, realized that they were very disconnected from their customers. The employees most connected to the customers were the "blue shirts," the sales staff who worked in thousands of stores across the country. Koelling and Bendt began to collaborate on an idea to capture the knowledge and learn from store employees. They created a platform for conversation to occur called Blue Shirt Nation. Through this platform, the sales staff suggest improvements, learn about new products, and network with like-minded employees across the organization and across the country. These employees are encouraged to openly communicate and bring their concerns directly to leadership. Koelling claims the only rule to Blue Shirt Nation is "don't be stupid." Employees are held responsible for what they post, and participation is not required.

The ideas generated by Blue Shirt Nation have helped create new programs for Best Buy. Employees are constantly suggesting ideas for store and customer satisfaction improvement. A great Blue Shirt Nation success story concerns Nick Pfeifer, an avid gamer who had great ideas to improve customer services for gamers, some of Best Buy's most loyal customers. He posted these ideas on the gaming section of Blue Shirt Nation. Corporate listened to his thoughts and paid to fly him from his Colorado Springs store to headquarters. Nick had multiple meetings with Best Buy executives, during which it was decided that his ideas would revolutionize how the store sells and markets video games. Imagine if Nick had only communicated his idea within his own store. Without an infrastructure to send the best ideas to the top, these thoughts would have never gained any traction. Most importantly, Best Buy was able to obtain these great ideas not from a million-dollar market research campaign or through the work of consultants, but through its own store employee (Haugen, 2009).

You do not have to be a high technology company or have a fleet of developers in order to create a revolutionary social media–based communication plan. Pitney Bowes took a podcasting model and released it through the existing voicemail system. Pitney Bowes, the company best known for creating postage meters, sought to align itself as a company in constant growth through acquisitions and mergers. Between 2001 and 2006, it acquired 53 smaller companies in order to complete its aggressive growth strategy. These acquisitions led to a fractured company in serious need of a means of uniting employees to achieve the common goals of a "one company approach." Internal communication was used to drive this strategy, led by Vice President of Employee Communications Rob Hallam. Hallam achieved unification primarily by creating a global communication project called "Universal Reach," which was designed to support and maintain a unified corporate culture. "Our goal is to provide 90 percent message accessibility within our key customer facing audiences," Hallam states. "The biggest challenge is integrating our online communication infrastructure which has nine different voicemail systems operating across the world and multiple e-mail and web platforms. We're pulling all that together to provide better reach" (AllBusiness, 2006, p. 2).

Social Media as Communication Management

Hallam broadcasts a weekly audio message called a Power Talk to employee voicemails throughout the world. Employees without voicemail receive these broadcasts by newsletter or through staff meeting listening opportunities. These broadcasts include the CEO and other top executives and seek to educate managers and employees about all of the products and services that Pitney Bowes offers. This knowledge has created many opportunities for employees to cross-sell products based on customer needs. While this model sounds primitive, it is important to realize that social media tools do not need to be flashy in order to be successful. Pitney Bowes leveraged a model commonly called podcasting through its corporate voicemail system. In the end, it created a more unified staff across a globally diverse corporation driven by acquisition (AllBusiness, 2006).

External and internal communication efforts can increase engagement through the use of social media sites. Content generated for external audiences commonly takes the form of marketing messages, but these messages gain traction through sharing features innately present in social media. Interested parties are able to "like" or "re-tweet" messages to their communities to increase awareness, which can directly lead to increased sales. Social media enhances internal communication in order to increase employee retention and unify staff behind a common mission and goal. While the methods and tools may change depending on the organizational structure, the sharing inherent to social media sites is rapidly changing the way organizations communicate both internally and externally.

Chapter 6
Social Media as a Marketing Tool

Children's Hospital

In early 2009, Jesse Stremcha was hired as ephilanthropy specialist for Children's Hospital and Clinics of Minnesota. Stremcha worked with the digital media team to immediately begin using Facebook, Twitter, a blog, and YouTube as marketing tools. Children's patients are the best representatives of and ambassadors for the brand, so the digital team looks to connect with donors by publishing stories about patients and their experiences at Children's. They have found YouTube videos can be much more effective than just press releases as viewers can see and hear from the families helped by Children's.

In just a few months, the team's efforts generated 4,000 "likes" on Children's Facebook account. About half of these are active in any given month. The Children's team integrates all social media channels to amplify the others and to deliver a consistent message about the brand. Children's also connects patients and families with other organizations such as CaringBridge, a website for chronically ill people.

Stremcha uses these channels to build Children's place in the "online ecosystem of healthcare and philanthropy in the Twin Cities." He also uses it to aid the fundraising capacity of Children's. Stremcha's efforts have resulted in invitations to speak around the country on online fundraising and healthcare social media marketing.

Historical Context

Social media has created new rules for marketing. Some might say that social media has radically shifted the way marketing is done and marketing budgets are allocated. This is true, but the science of marketing is a new science that has always been evolving. Social media marketing is just the next phase of its evolution. Twenty-five percent of display ads today in the United States are now on Facebook. In 2010, packaged goods giant Proctor & Gamble announced that it was reallocating a large portion of its advertising funds from TV and other traditional advertising toward social media. This is not the first company to do so, nor will it be the last.

Elements of marketing have been present for hundreds of years. Vendors verbally hawked their wares in town squares and marketplaces in the middle ages, and prostitutes and churches alike used word of mouth to spread their messages. Before print media was widespread, verbal advertising was the sole means of selling. Snake oil salespeople in the American west peddled their wares off the back of trucks in small towns.

Social Media as a Marketing Tool

Traveling salesmen sold commercial and industrial goods in the west in the 19th and 20th centuries. Sometimes they carried their products with them (like milkmen); other times they took orders. The first widespread marketing tool in America was the Sears catalog, a thick book of products. This catalog was one of the most coveted books a household could possess, and, outside of the Holy Bible, one of the most ubiquitous.

In the 20th century, marketing changed with the available technology. Beginning in the 1930s, radio ads pushed products, followed by TV ads, supporting the television industry. Marketing departments began to form in large corporations in the 1950s and 1960s, unifying and coordinating their advertising and sales efforts. These departments regulated pricing strategies, print and other media strategies, product/service line strategies, and distribution channel management. Eventually, they also conducted market research, divided markets into segments, and worked on strategic direction with corporate management.

In the 1990s, corporations sprouted small "online marketing" departments or positions to manage internet marketing, then a fledgling function. Other start-up online companies grew out of nowhere. Many of these flamed out in the dot.com bust of 2001–2002. Others, like eBay and Amazon.com, evolved into online giants. The rise of internet marketing, along with the advances in collaborative technologies, set the stage for social media marketing.

Goals of Marketing

The goals of marketing are fairly simple and clear: sell to new customers, sell more products or services to existing customers, generate referrals, retain customers, and build a strong brand. Marketing activities must act in unison to achieve these goals. Traditional and social media marketing efforts must work together and reinforce each other. CBS shouldn't tweet just because ABC or NBC does. The use of Twitter has to fit into CBS's central marketing goals.

The Old and New Rules of Marketing

Factor of Advertising: AVENUES	
OLD RULES	**NEW RULES**
TV, radio, press releases, billboards, newspapers, magazines	Blogs, social media sites, micro-blogs, interactive collaborative sites
Factor of Advertising: DIRECTION	
One-way: we pound you with "buy" messages	Two-way: we discuss
Factor of Advertising: WHEN	
During our pre-determined ad campaign	At the precise moment that you want it

Factor of Advertising: TONE	
You will buy because you need it, says I	Let's discuss your options and needs
Factor of Advertising: CONTENT	
Sizzle of the steak	Useful and balanced content; beginning of a conversation
Factor of Advertising: SUCCESS FACTOR	
Creativity	Depth of conversation
Factor of Advertising: WHO	
The masses	You alone

The Six Cs

In traditional marketing books, the "four Ps" were king: promotion, product, place, and price. In later years, a fifth P, people or customer service, was added. In social media marketing, we suggest evaluating the six Cs: conversation, community connection, conductivity, coherency, competition, and companion marketing.

Conversation

One-way and interruption-oriented marketing (buy, buy, buy!) has become a sort of conversation or dialogue through blogs, Twitter, and Facebook.

Under the old rules we yelled "Buy, buy, buy" from billboards, magazine ads, TV commercials, and other media outlets for all to hear. We yelled and screamed in order to get "percentage of ear" or *someone somewhere* to pay a little attention to our message versus the 3,000+ other advertising messages that potential consumers received each day.

A conversation has give-and-take, it has two willing sides. A conversation incorporates feedback and has action items. Companies today have conversations with proponents as well as disgruntled users. Markets evolve from buy-and-sell transactions to give-and-take conversations. The acts of selling, customer service, and marketing research all become conversations.

Service recovery is a conversation. For instance, many companies now employ people or contract with outside firms to scan the social media daily to find people and organizations who express negative opinions about their products. Once they find them, usually online, they engage in conversations as to the nature of the problem and attempt to resolve it. This process is often called "cleaning up digital dirt." Comcast regularly scans Twitter for actionable complaints and has customer service representatives who respond to these complaints.

In 2010, Logos Bible Software (online company) sold $300,000 of product during the traditional "Black Friday" with a simple Facebook promotion. The promotion, conceived and executed just four days before the weekend, simply asked Facebook fans which three products they wanted to see on sale during the three-day weekend. Potential customers were responded to individually with the sale prices of those items. These customers were given 48 hours to buy at these prices. Word spread through Facebook, tweets, retweets, and Logos gained hundreds of new Facebook fans and Twitter followers. They also sold 2,000 products, and sales were up 300% from the prior year. This case shows the nimbleness, agility, and word-of-mouth potential of social media marketing (Hibbard, 2011).

Another example involves technical conversations. Indium has 14 of its chemists involved in blogging on highly technical products (Hanson, 2010). The company supplies short bios and pictures, and suddenly there are real people behind their products. Who says engineers and chemists cannot be front people? Indium has made this possible.

Marketers have always craved a conversation with consumers or potential consumers. Using social media tools, now they have one. Large companies, like Dell Computer, have a Chief Listening Officer as part of their C-suite executives. These professionals sift through all the conversations with customers to mine the important nuggets of knowledge from this information.

Community Connection

Web 2.0 is extremely targeted. Specific groups are reached through specific means. Amazon.com knows your previous purchases; they send you lists of books that are similar to your previous purchases. Ferret owners receive all the latest information on ferret breeding, maintenance, and the love and care of ferrets through blogs of user groups. If you have registered your Twitter account with your neighborhood Starbucks, you will receive a tweet telling you that between 2:00 p.m. and 4:00 p.m., you can get $1 off of a grande caramel mocha.

Check out how the Washington Redskin football team used social media during the 2010 season. Redskin fans were encouraged to check in on Foursquare when they attended a game (over 30,000 did so). Once "checked in," their names were entered in a sweepstakes. These fans also "checked in" to 30 different local bars and restaurants that were Redskin friendly. These locations were available for fans when the Redskins were out of town. In this targeted use of Foursquare, the Washington Redskins used social media to build a community.

Under the new rules, the goal of marketing efforts is to create a community, or tribe, around your product or service. As an example, imagine you sell World War II relics. You have your products displayed on a website and write a blog about issues and new insights about World War II relics. Members of your community respond to your blog, and you have a link to the World War II relic museum and sponsor trips to it. You sponsor an annual conference and gather speakers, and you feature links to the stories and work of these World War II speakers on your website. Your blog and website also have links to other history blogs. You organize user groups in large communities and help avid collectors connect with each other through social media sites. You create an album of World War II pictures using Flickr or Picasa. By doing all of these things, you have organized a community with yourself at the center. If you recommend a book, your followers will buy it and you will receive a kickback. They rely on you because they receive news and information about upcoming events through you first and your community gathered around you.

eBay is a social media site that defines itself as a community creating communities. Buyers and sellers of 1947 Roadster paraphernalia come together through eBay to buy and sell these artifacts. They get to know each other through the bidding and selling process. They build trust through these transactions. eBay has created a community through mutual client passion, buying, and selling. One of the successful survivors of the dot.com bust, eBay has harnessed social media tools for that end: community.

Online communities are useful catalysts of social connection; they can also aid in mass collaboration. "Crowd sourcing" is the name of the process of getting input on a subject from a variety of people. An individual can define an issue on a blog or a social media website and ask for others to respond. Whereas marketing research used to be a drawn-out laborious process, crowd sourcing can be fast. Another benefit of this form of information gathering is the two-way conversation it creates. In addition to the information the question-asker receives, those responding to the questions gain access to responses of others.

Larger communities have been coined "ecosystems" by social media gurus. Your larger community includes competitors, blog readers, collaborators, stores, providers, and experts—all those concerned with your interest. These ecosystems are constantly shifting. In the old marketing days, the "us" or "them" mentality prevailed. Now, we're part of an ecosystem including "competitors" and social media tools, which allows for a deeper understanding of the totality of that ecosystem.

Conductivity

Technically, conductivity is a material's ability to conduct an electrical current. Metaphorically, conductivity is the ability of a message to move through channels or groups of people. Transparency is the ability to be seen. Transparency breeds openness, communication, and accountability. Social media tools put companies under the lime light more intensely than ever before. Corporate activities can be seen by few or transmitted to the masses. Social media tools pull back the curtain to reveal the inner workings of the great Wizard of Oz, and people realize that he may not be so great.

In the world of social media, brand and culture become two sides of a fast spinning coin. We see both sides of the coin in this world of conductivity and transparency. If both sides of the coin do not match, the world soon knows. If you tout a brand as a wonderful and brilliant product or service, but the employee or customer experience relayed through social media platforms reveals discontent, your flaws will blare like an out-of-tune aria.

In the "experience economy," social media is expected to provide a "wow" experience. Customers and would-be customers anticipate having fun on websites, blogs, and Twitter. In the culture of social media, where conductivity and transparency are paramount, organizations cannot hide behind marketing material, front offices, or billing departments. This "wow" experience does not necessarily have to come in the form of something extreme, such as a customer bungee jump, but can come in many forms. A "wow" experience can be

- an online helper who not only solves problems, but anticipates and solves potential problems;
- a quick connection;

- a timely recommendation for other products and services ("We have found that customers who have bought _____ also like _____."); and
- a humor break in the middle of the day. (The best humor is poking fun at oneself—check out the "timeline" on Trader Joe's website.)

Netflix's corporate culture presentation on Slideshow (a presentation-driven social media site) is a brilliant illustration of the transparency and conductivity. While many PowerPoints and employee handbooks are dull or boring, Netflix's presentation comes to life as a casual conversation. As the presentation relays the company's values, mission, and policies, and the evolution of its vacation policy ("take a vacation when you need one"), the viewer feels like he or she is part of a conversation with the company itself. After watching these 100-plus slides, who would *not* want to work with or do business with Netflix?

Coherency

Following closely behind conductivity is coherency. Social media tools make it essential to have coherency in your customer relationship management (CRM) approach. Inconsistency or incoherency will not go unnoticed by web scrutinizers. Would-be customers will realize the discrepancies that emerge from your espoused values ("We put our customers first and foremost!") and real values ("I have called XYZ Company five times and they have yet to respond, and my new air conditioner remains broken in the 100 degree heat!").

With many platforms from which to broadcast a message, extra effort must be made to ensure that these messages are congruent and consistent. They cannot be signs pointing in different directions—they must build on each other. There must be congruence between traditional marketing and social media marketing.

A good example of this phenomenon is the author and brand Seth Godin. His first best-selling book, *Permission Marketing: Turning Strangers into Friends and Friends into Customers* (1999), was followed with other books, a website, blog, podcasts, and workshops. All of these outlets have the personal stamp of Seth: clear, simple ideas; a penchant for breaking the rules and looking at things differently; and an aim to take meaning out of situations. Each media platform hosts a conversation with Godin's audience as if each fan is one-on-one with the author.

Competition

Who are your competitors? What are they doing in the marketplace? These two questions have perplexed marketers for years—nothing new here. Marketing researchers elicit information from consumers to answer these questions. In fact, after the fall of the Berlin Wall, many cold warrior spies morphed into corporate espionage and marketing research specialists. These specialists did not ferret out positions of enemy nuclear submarines, but of future positioning of competitive product offerings. Yes, their jobs are less exciting, but not as dangerous!

Social media allows you to examine your competitor's movements much faster, and vice versa. Transparency is reciprocal. The same organization that monitors your digital dirt monitors your competitor's market movements and digital dirt. Walmart can see what Target detractors are saying and respond quickly with a marketing campaign to make use of that weakness. McDonald's can take advantage of a competitor's struggle with *e coli* and tout its own cleanliness practices.

One can use all major social media tools to examine competitors. YouTube videos can indicate strategy. Facebook friends and Twitter followers may be customers and clients of one's competitors. The Twitter tool Tweepi displays details of one's Twitter followers, including biographical information. This competitive information would be a great project for a young marketing intern and a great beginning of a social media forensics career.

Beyond seeing marketing moves more quickly, the competitive landscape comes into focus more quickly with Web 2.0. Starbucks' main competition used to be other high-end coffee shops; now it is McDonald's and SuperAmerica. The principal competition of St. Paul, Minnesota's Concordia University used to be other small liberal arts colleges in the state; now it is for-profit universities like Capella, Rasmussen, Argosy, and the University of Phoenix. As the sands of the competitive landscape shift, organizations must use social media tools to stay abreast of competitive activities.

Companion Marketing

Companion (sometimes called affiliate) marketing is an offshoot of community; it involves cross marketing into someone else's community. For instance, most successful blogs promote a list of their own favorite blogs and reference them readily for their readers. Companion marketing involves crossing "your" community with "their" community in search of commonality between the two. A forerunner to companion marketing is the trend of one nonprofit organization selling their "list" to another. In this case, however, consumers rarely have a say in where their email or home addresses are shared. In companion marketing, participants choose whether to join adjacent communities or not.

In some cases, companion marketing works on a quid pro quo basis. You promote my blog, and I will promote your blog. Companion marketing can also mean placing paid advertisements on your blog. You might charge a monthly fee or a commission for anything sold through your blog. The blogger takes no ownership of the product, but has a relationship with a community that he or she is willing to share. Let us assume that a blogger who writes about eccentric dogs has 15,000 ardent dog lovers reading his blog regularly. If I sell premium dog food, advertising on his website is a golden opportunity.

> **Uses of Blogs in Marketing**
> - To build a reputation, expertise, or legitimacy in a field
> - To participate in an industry-wide conversation
> - To solicit feedback that may be good but hard on your product/service offerings
> - To connect with other conversations and communities in a general field; to connect conversations, communities, and relationships

Differentiating Your Marketing Approach

Here is the pitfall: Everyone has a Facebook page, writes a blog (110 million blogs at last count), tweets about specials, and has those funny little symbols next to their trade name (the more symbols, the cooler). This means you have to be different. Walmart did not situate their locations next to Sears or Kmart. They chose small rural communities that the other big players had left behind. Amazon did not grow popular by building a better bookstore.

Harley Davidson did not necessarily create a better bike; they created a better brand (and a huge tribe of avid tattooed supporters). Home Depot did not grow by trying to be a better hardware store, but by creating a new *class* of store. So, how are you going to do the same? Copying the approach of your competitor is not going to leapfrog you forward.

The seminal work *Blue Ocean Strategy: How to Create Uncontested Market Space and Make Competition Irrelevant* (Kim and Mauborgne, 2005) reveals the advantages of choosing uninhabited blue ocean waters, rather than competing in a red ocean of bloody, shark-eat-shark competition. Authors W. Chan Kim and Renée Mauborgne suggest that organizations examine the industry offerings and remake their own by *creating*, *raising*, *lowering*, or *eliminating* according to what else is out there. By using these four screens, you create something new and different and, therefore, compete in a blue ocean rather than in the red one. This notion becomes your marketing challenge over the next several years. How do you create a cohesive tribe of customers and clients with your organization at the center?

Concluding Social Media Marketing Tips

Although there is much disagreement about the *how*s, *why*s, and *what for*s of social media marketing, some rules are agreed upon:

- The horse is out of the barn; social media marketing is here to stay.
- Social media marketing can be used for ecommerce, branding, marketing research, customer retention, and leading generations.
- Stop talking and start listening. Capture all the data you can and have a person (or people) organize it.
- Web 2.0 is a democratic tool that recognizes participants equally.
- If you embark on a unified marketing campaign, what is in it for the consumer? Social media is an exchange; it is not one way.
- You will receive feedback whether you want it or not. First, grow and change from the feedback. Second, respond to the feedback in appropriate ways.
- Your brand is not necessarily something you can craft with a logo and cute design. Your brand is the sum total of your customer and employee experiences. For better or worse, they will be broadcast throughout Web 2.0. While you can mold, influence, and shape your brand, you do not have 100% control.
- Marketing as an interruption is out; do not encroach on the customer's time. Let the customer do the encroaching.

- Social media is part of a total marketing approach; it needs to be integrated with the other more traditional marketing tactics: supply chain, pricing, selling, and strategy.
- Connecting with people today creates buyers tomorrow.
- Marketing as "selling" has evolved into marketing as "sharing."
- You may not own your own brand like you used to; the customers often take ownership of the brand in the world of social media marketing.

Chapter 7
Social Media as an Innovation Tool

Innovation through Deep Listening

A nutrition company (let's call it XYZ Corp) wanted to extend its product line. The company already had a very large market share in nutritional supplements for children with a particular kind of disability. XYZ hired a product design company to help. The design company found a handful of households with children suffering from this kind of disability. Teams of professionals from both companies visited these stay-at-home parents in their homes and observed and listened to these parents as they worked in their kitchens.

The acute listening skills of the marketing and design professionals helped them understand the deeper needs and desires of these parents for their disabled children. After their visit, these professionals returned to the design company's office. There, they pooled their observations and what they learned about their target market. Using this information, they created new products and services aimed at this market.

These steps, although roughly outlined above, constitute a proven process for innovation. Unfortunately, the innovation process can sometimes be expensive and time-consuming. It involves finding the right potential customers and listening and observing them deeply. After gleaning information, a team then uses creative methods to develop new product ideas. How can social media tools make the process of innovation faster and/or less costly?

Social Media and Innovation

Social media is an innovation, or series of innovations; can it also be used to create innovations? Yes, social media can be a powerful innovation tool. Social media brings customers into the conversation. These tools can make meaning of consumer wants and desires, and create value-added products or services for these consumers.

What is innovation? Innovation is the successful introduction of something new or different. Innovation can be a minor change like the downsizing of cell phones. Innovation can be something radically different like the iPod. Innovation can be the combination of two existing items like bookstores and coffee shops or cars and cup holders. Innovation creates new wealth and often drives economies. Innovations can be huge like the "Chunnel" (the tunnel under the English Channel connecting England and France) or small like entrepreneurs in Mexico who make sandals out of used automobile tires.

As a result of increased global competition, organizations have to become more innovative. If they do not, they will lose market dominance and market share. Nonprofit organizations have to be innovative in order to do more with less. Companies need to come up with new and different product and service offerings in order to keep customers happy. Government organizations need to be innovative in order to solve global problems like pollution, poverty, crime, and disease—and usually with fewer resources.

Most innovations occur because groups of people creatively collaborate on mutual issues, products, or problems. The myth of the lone inventor, or innovator, is truly a myth. Social media tools allow for more communication than has been possible in the past. Physically separated people can work together more efficiently than ever before. The great inventor Thomas Edison had a dozen or so engineers working on his bench, shoulder-to-shoulder. Social media tools can create the same effect even if the engineers are not shoulder-to-shoulder; these tools enhance creative collaboration. Social media tools allow diverse resources and ideas to collect and combine as never before. Diversity breeds innovation, and social media tools allow for much diversity.

The Innovative Mind

What is the innovative mind?

- The innovative mind is **curious**: Leonardo da Vinci would find seashells on top of mountains and ask, "Why?" Innovators look at imperfect products and ponder whether or not something can be done to improve them. One Seattle innovator, Roger Johnson, looked at lobsters' eyes curiously, researched them, and invented a heating device from their operating principles. *In social media, bloggers need to be curious about the responses of followers.*

- The innovative mind questions and **challenges assumptions**: Why does this process require 14 steps and 25 days? Why should a car need gasoline to move? Why does one need to live near a college campus in order to earn a degree? *How can social media connect the right people for the right project?*

- The innovative mind is **restless**, open to new ideas, and not content with the status quo: How can I improve this or that? If I tinker long enough, I will find a better way for this to be done. *How will social media evolve to help solve problems?*

- The innovative mind is a **systems** thinker: An innovator who is a systems thinker sees how parts fit together as a whole. An innovator sees the world with a wide-angle rather than a telephoto lens. *How can I use social media tools to create market synergy?*

- The innovative mind engages in **convergent and divergent** thinking: In divergent thinking, the innovator discovers many possibilities and options. With convergent thinking, the innovator narrows down the possibilities to a few or even one. *How do you keep encouraging the many ideas when you only run with the few?*

- The innovative mind is **persistent**: Most great inventors or innovators experience many failures before success. Thomas Edison's team developed over 900 renditions of the light bulb that did not work. *How can we persistently glean the few great ideas from the many that social media channels will bring us?*

An excellent case study on innovation and social media is IBM. IBM uses a decentralized approach to social media. Instead of the Marketing Department being in complete control of social media messages and content, IBM allows its employees to use these tools. The results are impressive: 17,000 blogs, 200,000 blog users, thousands of external blog users, and 200,000 LinkedIn sites.

More impressively, 500,000 people have participated in "crowd-sourcing jams," the equivalent of asynchronous open brainstorming sessions. These sessions have identified the 10 best incubator projects. These were funded with $100 million. The company reports billions in revenue from these efforts. Innovation author, Clayton Christensen, calls this "one big collaborative experiment" (Hibbard, 2010, para. 27).

Behaviors Leading to Innovation

Babies come from storks, right? It is not easy to say where innovation comes from; it emanates from many diverse sources. Social media tools are able to enhance some of these sources.

- **Getting into Another Box:** The popular maxim is "get out of the box." In fact, many innovations come from switching boxes. Henry Ford sent two of his engineers to the stockyards in Chicago to observe how hogs were butchered on an assembly line. Ford was reported as saying "what is good enough for hogs is good enough for cars." When developing a tracking system for ex-felons, the state of Minnesota studied Target's inventory tracking system for development ideas.

    Social media tools allow for getting into another box more rapidly. Because of the immediacy of the communication through social media tools, individuals and groups can enter "other boxes" instantaneously. Some governmental organizations put their strategic plans on shared sites online. If you are appointed to create a strategic plan for an urban county, consider perusing Minnesota's Dakota County website rather than reinventing the wheel. With the transparency produced by social media tools, jumping into other boxes is easier than ever.

- **By Mistake and Observation:** The Post-it Note emanated from glue that did not quite stick, polio was invented from a contaminated experiment, the microwave was conceived when a scientist's candy bar melted in his pocket as he walked past a magnetron machine. After the initial accident, as in these cases and many others, acute observation was necessary in order to make a connection between the failure and a new, useful product.

  Social media tools can help with the dissemination of information about mistakes and accidents. A multitude of people can hear about these failures and then connect them to new possibilities. Special-interest blogs disseminate new information with rapid speed. For instance, user groups of elaborate software, cleaning chemicals, or video games share insights concerning what does or does not work. Users provide workarounds for other users through these mechanisms.

- **Through Big Events and Dislocations:** In mid-2010, a major oil spill polluted the coast of the Gulf of Mexico. Pretty soon, the details of the problem were being broadcast across the internet. Websites popped up with blogs where people across the globe posited ideas for solving the problem. Saving the gulf became the challenge not just of British Petroleum or the United States government, but of anyone who cared to help.

- **By Scientific and Engineering Breakthroughs:** As more and more companies embrace open source innovation, scientific, medical, and technical breakthroughs spread faster. Recent studies suggest that most new innovations are created by collaborations between universities, corporations, foundations, and governmental agencies. In order for these breakthroughs to happen, new knowledge sharing has to occur. Collaborative tools and communication devices facilitate this need. In addition, these tools allow for more diverse entities to be part of the innovation process.

The Innovation Process

Various types of innovation processes are practiced by organizations. Most of them, however, have these steps in common: framing the issue, data dump, gathering information, crowdsourcing, organizing the information, prototype development, prototype refinement and evaluation, and implementation. Let's see how these steps can be enhanced by using social media.

- **Framing the Issue:** What is the problem/challenge/issue at hand? Are we trying to build a better bicycle? Are we trying to reduce the waste emitted by our plant? Do we want to bring a new product to market in 160 days rather than a year? Is this the right issue to address?

Social media tools allow inputs from entities across the globe. Perhaps you quickly need input from your marketing professionals in Asia. You could have a three-way teleconference between Asia, Europe, and the Americas—or you could set up a combination of shared computer questions and blog-type arena in order to bounce ideas back and forth. Or you could invite insights through a Twitter post. With shared computer space, issues can be framed and agreed upon.

- **Primary Data Dump:** What do you know about the problem right now? Many stakeholders can take part in this preliminary process. In a traditional world, participants would be in the same room, and reports might have been circulated. Facts, figures, ideas, and conjectures would be written on the board. In a dispersed world, internet collaboration tools like Basecamp, Central Desktop, and Dropbox provide a platform for group data dumps (many pieces of information from many sources shared among many people). Dispersed populations can add to documents and co-create documents at the same or different times.

In this case, social media tools allow for a wider group of participants in the process. According to the principles put forth by the classic *Wisdom of the Crowds* (Surowiecki, 2005), the more diverse the contributing population, the better the process. More thoughts are better than few.

- **Data Gathering:** During the previous step, gaps between existing and desired information became apparent. Sometimes these gaps will be significant; other times, the gaps will be minor. These gaps can be filled by observations, questionnaires, or other methods of research.

- **Crowdsourcing:** Crowdsourcing has become a popular method of gaining much input from external sources. One can pose a question on a blog or social media platforms like Facebook or Twitter. All of one's followers can respond with input, sources, new angles on the issue, or places to find an answer. Instead of one person digging in the bowels of a library or a database, an entire network and its network of sources are available quickly and efficiently.

- **Data Organizing:** A copious amount of data needs to be organized. A co-located team might rearrange Post-it Notes on a wall to build themes. Software exists to accomplish this, and dispersed teams can use this software together. Even if elaborate software is not used, other social media tools can enable prompt communication so that participants no longer have to wait to be together to execute this step of the process. The social media concept of "tagging" (hashtags) helps associate words or themes with objects for easier organization.

- **Initial Prototype Development and Experimentation:** Rapid prototyping is a must in this fast-changing, competitive business world. Organizations must learn how to quickly introduce products into the marketplace and then tweak them to perfection if necessary. Again, collaborative software is available that can help geographically dispersed people build prototypes together. This phase is much faster because of the social media tools available to obtain feedback from stakeholders.

- **Prototype Tweaking and Evaluation:** A company can develop several prototypes and put them on its website, available to all constituents. The constituents can vote for the prototype that they prefer and add comments for the developers. The company does not have to abide by the voting results, but the process might reveal valuable facts concerning their clientele's thoughts. Some of the feedback might even help develop the prototype.

Two caveats need to be mentioned here: First, this type of activity might tip your hand to your competition. Second, there is the potential for your competition to contaminate your results by voting and commenting. The problem with open sourcing is that it is open—open to competitors, jokesters, and mean people. As with much of social media or online activity, you often do not really know who is on the other end of a comment.

- **Implementation:** When you introduce many new products and services, social media marketing can be a promotional device. If your product is aimed at seniors, you might skip this kind of marketing. As the chapter on social media marketing suggests, many helpful innovative tools are available.

Area for Innovation	Potential Impact of Social Media
Supply Chain	Social media tools allow for tighter communication in supply chains.
Front of the House	Presence: Where are you? If you are a mobile food cart, you can tweet your location. Foursquare can tell others who has entered.
Product/Service	Social media's collaborative tools allow geographically dispersed inventors to work together.
Image/Brand	Your brand can be broadcasted through a variety of tools all at once. Your presence can be ubiquitous.
Culture	Your culture is transparent and must match your brand promise. Brand/culture must be two sides of one coin.
Work Processes	Dispersed groups can work together more easily by using collaborative tools to improve work processes.

Social Media as an Innovation Tool

Value Capture	Social media channels can capture user input and find holes in the value chain that might point to profitable services.
Total Solutions	When you do not have a total solution for a potential client, social media tools allow you to collaborate more quickly with others whom you can pattern with.
Customer Segment	Different customers use different communication tools; you can match these more efficiently using social media tools.
Customer Experience	Feedback is easier with social media tools. You can easily mine comments from happy and unhappy customers through social media channels.

Ghost Hunting: A Case

Say that you have always been intrigued by dead people and you wish to build a business around your interest. You have dabbled in ghost hunting and you are convinced that there is a growing interest in this topic (do not quit your day job yet). How can you build an innovative business around your passion?

First, ask yourself, who are the key players in this industry? You search the internet for similar businesses. You find a couple blogs and start posting comments; you are beginning the process of establishing yourself as an expert. You attend the "Ghostbusters" yearly conference, and you talk to everyone who will give you the time of day. You find out their favorite blogs, RSS feeds, and likes and dislikes. You collect Facebook and LinkedIn contacts and stay in touch with your new network. You set up an RSS feed around the subject of ghost hunters. While doing all of this, you are listening acutely to the chatter about ghosts and ghost-chasing.

Based on your observations and research, you conclude that many other impassioned ghost hunters are doing what you want to do and some of them, for free. Some of the more enterprising ghost hunters make money with online stores and workshops. Other ghost-lovers lead tours. Some even hold séances. In fact, at first blush, the world seems flush with people who want to make money off of departed souls. What to do?

Innovation is about connections. So you start looking for other angles through trend hunting on social media. Through Digg, Reddit, Quora, and other sources, you find many others writing about the aging of the population in the United States—the baby boomers reaching retirement age, older people reflecting on their legacies, and people just generally trying to make meaning of their lives. Because of social media tools, you have much more information at your fingertips than ever before. You create mind maps where you make connections out of this information—it is your job to make meaning out of this raw data.

You discover a unique connection: a service for baby boomers as they observe and go through the transition of loved ones. This service includes helping loved ones understand the dynamics of transition, getting in touch with loved ones after they have made the transition, building shrines for the departed, and holding workshops on making meaning of death, forgiveness, and the afterworld. You decide to build a prototype website with these services highlighted. You use all of these aforementioned social media tools to build yourself a platform with a blog listing links to other ghost-hunter blogs, websites, and ghost-busting stores. You continue to build your industry connections and link your social media to theirs through LinkedIn, Twitter, and various RSS feeds.

Conclusion

Social media tools make it possible to engage in meaningful dialogues with customers and potential customers. These dialogues can be fertile ground for "aha's" leading to innovations. For instance, the specialty chemical giant (soaps) Unilever has created an online, social media–based, consumer-driven product development process. Because of social media tools, Unilever has extensive conversations with consumers at the front end of the development cycle. These tools allow for faster and more robust sharing by individuals and groups who are not standing next to each other, like Edison's engineers. In a way, these social media tools have been developed at a time when they are needed the most. Innovation is necessary to solve the economic, social, and environmental problems faced across the globe.

Chapter 8
Creating People Partnerships Using Social Media

Kiva

Kiva is a nonprofit organization that connects people who have money with people who need money. It uses social media to create social good. Borrowing as little as $25, borrowers have financed small and home-based businesses in developing countries. A woman in Tajikistan started a home sewing business. A man in Bulgaria named Angel opened his own bicycle repair store and successfully repaid his $850 loan in 12 months. Kiva was so successful at first that it ran out of borrowers. The company posts YouTube videos on its website, has a Facebook app, and harnesses Twitter to build relationships with its lending partners.

As you have undoubtedly realized by now, *connecting* is the purpose of social media. The people connections you build through social media are important because they help transform the ways you manage the people in your organization. Not only that, social media redefines for you the "in" in your organization. Suddenly, your partnership extends beyond employees and includes a larger community of people: potential and past employees and others who are in your industry and supply chain, as well as those who impact your organization. The beauty of social media is that all these people can actually become your **partners** and contribute to your organization's success and to your success as a manager. In this chapter, we focus on the people partnerships and organizational relationships created through social media.

Recruiting and Job Searching

Any good relationship begins with an introduction. Before the birth of social media, organizations navigated these professional introductions with recruiting campaigns. These took the form of recruiters or headhunters, job postings or job fairs. No more. The Harvard Business School Alumni Career Development site (Career Development, 2011) estimates that 65 to 85% of jobs are currently found by networking. While there are all kinds of ways to network, social networking provides effective opportunities for job seekers. Dan Schawbel (2009) identifies 10 sites as top social media networking opportunities.

Creating People Partnerships Using Social Media

Social Media Sites for Job Seekers

- **LinkedIn:** Create a profile that lists your experience and history. Connect with others who interest you. See first-, second-, and third-degree connections (friends, friends of friends, and friends of friends of friends) that might be useful.
- **Plaxo:** Create your profile, plus identify your social media presence and activities. Use the address book to handle contacts and map information. This site also connects directly to Simply Hired, a job aggregator or search engine.
- **Twitter:** Enhance your engagement on Twitter by including links to your blog, LinkedIn, or other profiles.
- **Jobster:** Interact with employers who have active job listings.
- **Facebook:** Look for direct job posts and join groups and fan lists of companies where you might like to work. Here you often connect with real people who do real hiring.
- **Craigslist:** Look here for small to midsized organizations with open positions.
- **MyWorkster:** Post a profile here if you are a college student or alumnus. This site also connects with **Indeed,** another job search engine and aggregator.
- **VisualCV:** Use this site to create a branded webpage of your own where you can include a wide variety of visual documentation.

> - **Jobfox:** Use this site to be paired with job openings that are compatible with your skillset and experience.
> - **Ecademy:** Another networking site similar to LinkedIn.

For both organization and job seeker, these social media networking opportunities save real money: the cost of recruiting and/or finders' fees. For recruiters and headhunters, these sites provide a pool of potential candidates who might have been previously overlooked. For everyone, this is a nonthreatening, noninvasive way to get a preliminary look at potential jobs and potential candidates. There is also an opportunity for transparency on both sides (potential employer and potential employee) that allows each to create a public "face" in the marketplace. This changes the initial relationship in a fundamental way. Instead of identifying a potential candidate whom an organization is willing to hire, or instead of a candidate identifying a potential employer for whom he or she is willing to work, both employers and candidates can (at least on a preliminary level) explore the potential for a good "fit." The higher the level of transparency, the more realistic this "fit" potential evaluation becomes. An additional benefit is the opportunity for continued connections for those who are not hired. This increases potential for long-lasting relationships that might be useful in the future.

One aspect that cannot be overlooked in social media networking is the importance of identifying your second- and third-degree connections. Your first-degree connections are people you already know one-to-one. When you are job searching or recruiting, these individuals will already connect you with their contacts. However, the second-degree (friends of friends) and third-degree (friends of friends of friends) connections are generally untapped resources that can multiply the impact of your search.

Employee Retention

Once a potential fit has been uncovered and an employee hired, social media can also improve employee retention. Connection increases retention, and social media is one way to increase connections. Some organizations promote connections through the use of an intranet site. Others use blogs. These allow employees to better understand the organizational culture and identify with it. In other words, it's easier to connect one's personal brand with the organizational brand. All of this builds trust at a fundamental level.

From an organizational perspective, monitoring the social media comments of your employees allows you to better understand their impressions of your organization. How good is the fit from your side? In what ways can you develop a better fit?

Social media is a way to better understand employees' needs and wants. For example, what kinds of incentives, rewards, or praise will most motivate employees to do their best?

Social media provides a variety of opportunities to let employees hear that they matter. Consider, for example, this statement from IBMers' blogs (n.d., para. 1):

> *A menu of expertise and insight from a passionate crowd.* As they'll tell you themselves, the opinions and interests expressed on IBMers' blogs are their own and don't necessarily represent this company's positions, strategies, or views. But that doesn't mean we don't want you to read them! Because they do represent lots of business and technology expertise you can't get from anyone else.

This is an incredible statement of corporate affirmation.

Employee ideas can matter, too, on social media sites. Companies capture these and use them for innovations. Likewise, employee successes can be noted on organization intranet sites. And, from an organization perspective, you might learn of employee success through employees' own postings that might typically go unnoticed.

Social media facilitates connections outside of your immediate boundaries. Maybe those boundaries are departmental or locational. Maybe they are functional. However, knowing others outside of the normal boundaries allows for the cross-pollination of ideas in interesting ways. Consider GE's initiative to create better marketing practices across the country. GE created an internal site called MarkNet in March 2010. In four months, more than 3,200 internal marketing professionals joined this online community. The community was organized around "hubs" of informational topics that included, among others, marketing communications, customer experience, value proposition, and pricing. The site provided a variety of ways to collaborate: moderated discussions, blogs, articles, video, a Twitter-like short message area, and conveniently linked internal documents. Jeffrey Cohen (2011) reports:

> In one of the clearest demonstrations of the value of the community, a marketer in one of the divisions was searching for a vendor to complete a marketing segmentation study. They posted a request for vendor recommendations on MarkNet. A team in another division, in another part of the world, had both the expertise and the time to complete the project for the cost of the team's time. This arrangement saved the company $250,000.

Clearly, there are financial advantages to collaboration. This contributes to employee feelings of success and increased retention.

In addition to financial returns, creativity returns are also noted due to social media connections. A study conducted by MIT researchers found that employees who connected through digital networks (i.e., social media) are 7% more productive than their colleagues (Pentland, 2009). Productivity begets success. Success results in more satisfied employees. More satisfaction yields greater employee retention.

Virtual Meetings

As organizations work on connecting their various partnerships, social media can provide substantial savings to an organization due to reduced meeting costs. As connections occur virtually, less travel is required. The use of Skype, YouTube, WebEx, and other media creates "face time" that is often the priority of physical meetings. Presentations can be delivered around the world in virtual space but in real time. When physical meetings are advantageous, social media can support these by providing opportunities for pre-meeting sharing of information. Furthermore, such pre-meeting sharing supports a variety of learning styles and helps all participants be more effective in contributing to the project. Social media also helps with recording thoughts, contributions, ideas, and conversations. Such recordkeeping can be useful for an organization's operations and planning.

Creating Partnerships

The word *partnership* implies some kind of equality. There is a working "together" rather than a working "for." Social media facilitates this kind of transaction on a variety of levels. First, participants meet in a neutral space, the virtual location of the social media site. There is no particular ownership or squatting right. Everyone is in the same virtual space. In addition, social media relationships tend to be more transparent and authentic, as well as occurring in real time. These characteristics contribute to a sense of equality in the partnership.

Note the fluidity of social media. Stakeholders change moment to moment as needed and can include those you already know plus those who are interested in your organization, product, or service. Thus, your stakeholder base is created by interest rather than defined boundaries—it is ever-changing. Crowdsourcing becomes real-time information when you solicit and receive input from your various social media interactions. On my current Facebook page, as of today, I have 95 wall posts on the initial page. Of these, 22 are from organizations rather than individuals. All of the organizational posts have comments. The comments to all of these are unsolicited, although in other instances there are very often invitations for feedback. Here is a lot of real information potentially received by these organizations, ranging from product accolades or complaints to a general like or dislike about the organization, product, or service. Real people, real time, real information. Should the same information appear again, others would engage. This gives you an almost limitless group of stakeholders that configures and reconfigures fluidly. Social media enables you to talk and listen—to really interact with those who are investing their time and thoughts.

Connections Outside Your Organization

Social media allows you to engage in partnerships outside your own organization. These outside partnerships might include industry participants, trade organizations, alumni groups, and more. At the onset, social media platforms allow you to easily manage your partnerships, especially when they appear as Facebook friends or Twitter followers. In addition, your own contacts allow you to reach second- and third-degree connections, because you have a ready introduction through mutual social media participation on a particular site. Disseminating information is easy, and event planning is expedited through various invitation mechanisms on the various sites. Even invitations become easier, as one posted invitation quickly reaches your intended audience and their connections. All of these characteristics increase the potential for connecting with more interested participants.

The Value of Partnerships

The investment you make in social media engagement and partnerships results in better employee "fits" in your organization, retaining successful employees, gaining important information relative to managing your organization, and receiving financial rewards. Identifying your priorities in managing these partnerships will help you recognize the best social media opportunities for meeting your objectives.

Chapter 9
Managing Strategy Using Social Media

The Humane Society of the United States

The Humane Society has a story to tell. It has animals to place. It has volunteers to support. It has donors to nurture. It shares information on animal health and welfare topics. It collects donations. It builds connections within its various communities. It communicates its business. Social media allows it to be who it is and do its work. Using blogs, Twitter, and Facebook, the Humane Society creates its business and interacts with its environment.

Strategy

Strategy, as managers already know, is more than planning. Plans come at the end of the strategy creation process. Strategic thinking is more robust and all-encompassing. In the most simple terms, strategic planning answers these questions:

- Who are we?
- Where are we?
- Where do we want to go?
- How do we get there?

You also need to examine the following:

- Your resources (what do you already have)
- Your customers or revenue generators (who will buy your services or products)
- Your operations (what do you need to do)
- Your performance (how will you measure your progress)

Central to your strategy is your organization's mission and vision. This needs to be internally and externally consistent with your organization's operations and culture. Social media provides an opportunity to gauge if they are communicated well and heard accurately. Monitoring internal organizational blogs and internal and external social media sites is extremely informative. Because social media communication is transparent and instantaneous, you can access a more accurate snapshot of what people inside and outside your organization think.

In addition to the immediacy and transparency afforded by social media, you also have the opportunity to draw information from a wider variety of constituencies. In the past, you may have been limited to work teams on the inside or focus groups from the outside. However, social media encourages quick, easy, and often anonymous contributions from employees, customers, other stakeholders, and even competitors. In this transparent and authentic environment, you can collect all kinds of information when you understand how and where to look for it. In addition, as you engage in the social media environment, you have the ability to invite and encourage others to join the discussion, thereby enabling the creation of more connections that allow the collection of more desired data.

Data Gathering for Strategic Planning

Social media allows you to gather data and understanding in specific key areas.

- **Competitor Analysis:** You can assess your industry to identify what others are doing and how their stakeholders and others are reacting to it. This raises the question: *Can you identify things **you** should be doing or not doing that would increase your competitive advantage?*

- **Supply Chain Understanding:** You can examine the operations and processes of those in your supply chain and see how these are perceived by their stakeholders. This raises the question: *Do the operations and processes in your supply chain support your organization in the best way possible?*

> - **Diversification Opportunities:** You can identify opportunities outside your current products or services and determine effectiveness from multiple perspectives. This raises the question: *Are there other products or services that you might be able to integrate into your organization for greater profitability?*

Answers to these questions determine additional data essential for the analysis that precedes strategic planning.

Defining a New and Real Time "Team"

An important consideration here is how the use of social media can change the definition of the "team" as you consider strategic implications. Before social media, your team often consisted of managers and executives. Obviously, their perspectives are limited by their ranks and experiences. Social media allows you to expand your team to include a wider variety of stakeholders and potential stakeholders. You hear from those whose opinions might be different but important. These perspectives might be important in allowing you to establish a previously overlooked competitive advantage. At the same time, you have the opportunity to monitor organizations in your supply chain or even your competition. You can learn what they are doing and determine the possible impact on your organization.

Not only is your team base broader in perspective, it is readily available in real time. Your team is readily accessible via any of the social media platforms. You might tweet a question about a possible product or solicit feedback on an ad from your Facebook friends. You might read the blogs of those in your industry to see what is being said about you or your competitors or visit YouTube to view videos related to your possible strategies. It is not one of these inputs, but a combination of multiple inputs that gives you real understanding of your environment and potential.

Monitoring and Celebrating

Part of strategic management includes recognizing and celebrating success. Social media can play a unique role in contributing to these efforts. As successes are identified, a variety of social media platforms can be used to share them. In addition, as you share via multiple platforms, you are reaching a wider variety of audiences. Short messages can be tweeted on Twitter. Facebook can contain both stories and links. YouTube can share video. Organizational blogs can highlight superstars. Success as perceived from the outside looking in can be monitored. What do industry bloggers say about your newest product? Are your customers sharing tweets about their latest experience? Do the outside views match your views from the inside? Answering these questions and analyzing the reasons for these answers will help you determine your next direction. If your discoveries are positive, you know to stay the course. If you find discrepancies, you are aware of the need to look for or create opportunities for improvement. Multiple constituents and multiple viewpoints help you develop a sound strategy based on both shared successes and identified opportunities.

Application to One Strategic Management Technique

Once you understand how social media applies, it is easy to extend its application throughout your processes. Let's quickly examine, for the sake of exploring social media's application, the Balanced Scorecard.

The Balanced Scorecard looks at your organization from four perspectives:

- **Financial:** Really examine your various statements, documents, and projections.

- **Customer:** Understand the value you are creating and for whom.

- **Internal Processes:** Look at what's going on inside your organization.

- **Learning and Growth:** Examine the current state and potential growth of
  - human capital;
  - information capital; and
  - organization capital.

From these perspectives, decision makers and strategists get a more balanced view of the organization that includes, but does not rely solely upon, financial measures. Social media can provide additional, valuable insights that were not previously available.

Financial

In addition to basis statements and projections, you can examine reactions to your numbers. What looks problematic to you on paper might be of no concern to stakeholders while a small number change on paper could cause uproar. By monitoring a variety of social media sites, you can determine the impact of your numbers. This will help you better understand what the numbers *mean* as you plan your strategies.

Customer

Social media allows you to broaden your perspectives to include both customers and potential customers. Monitoring a variety of sites provides multiple perspectives. Suppose you want to attract new customers to an existing product or to a new product. What are they already saying about these things? You can read existing posts or pose direct questions on your own sites. You can interact and dialogue with customers, existing and potential, through the entire spectrum of a product's life. This will help you understand more explicitly the value you are creating.

Internal Processes

If you have an internal blog or website, you can easily monitor the processes and your employees' reactions to them. However, even from outside social media sites, you can examine the impact of internal processes on your outside stakeholders.

Learning and Growth

How can you identify the need for, execution of, and results due to learning, particularly in the areas of human, information, and organization capital? Capital in these areas is often difficult to measure and therefore often difficult to understand. The stories told on social media sites provide ways to understand these capital structures even when they can't always be measured. Not only can you better understand the capital structures, you can authentically identify which of your stakeholders are impacted by each. Is need for information capital, for example, a challenge for your employees or your customers? Should your human resources department be looking toward more or less employee development training opportunities? As you follow various social media sites, you will begin to weave together the story of how each of these learning and growth areas influences your organization and how your organization influences them.

Innovation

One aspect of strategy that is always considered is innovation. Where do you get the ideas that will become integral to your new strategic objectives? Keeping your eyes open in the various social media venues will allow you to recognize not only opportunities identified by your stakeholders, but also innovations being discussed in relation to your competitors. Here is a place where the transparency and immediacy of social media really shine. You become an insider within your industry and your competition! Consider the explicit strategies for identifying innovative ideas employed by both Dell and Starbucks. Their approaches are very similar. Dell IdeaStorm (http://www.ideastorm.com) is a site that encourages the community to post ideas for Dell products and services. Launched in February, 2007, this site attracted 2,000 ideas in the first weeks. On the site, readers are encouraged to vote to promote or demote ideas and eventually see the adopted ideas in practice. Similarly, Starbucks has a My Starbucks Idea site (http://

mystarbucksidea.force.com). Areas on this site include Got an Idea?, View Ideas, and Ideas in Action. Both sites are incredible ways to tap into the notion of crowdsourcing, a concept where problem solving is distributed to a large body of interested parties and where the volume of participants tends to result in valuable responses.

Engaging with Your Supply Chain and Industry

No organization exists in isolation. In many ways, you are supported by your industry and/or business community while being supported by your supply chain and challenged by your competitors. In the environment of your industry, social media is instrumental in easily making connections that used to be difficult to navigate. Consider, for example, The Business Network Facebook application (http://www.facebook.com/apps/application.php?id=24249628048&ref=s). This networking site connects more than 100,000 small business owners with likeminded others.

Their stated objectives are to

- pursue goals. Set a goal and get support from the community, then leverage tools and get expert help.
- network and grow. Forge relationships and get new customers and leads.

- see results. Achieve your goals and realize dreams for your business.

Look for (or create) similar networking opportunities in your industry or community. These can enhance your operations and your connections, and reveal telling information in regards to the needs of your industry or community.

Final Word of Caution

This chapter has focused on the real and valuable ways that social media provides information that can fundamentally shape your strategic planning. The characteristics of transparency and immediacy make this information both interesting and valuable. However, keep in mind that this information can be misleading in very small doses. Is the customer who is complaining about your product on Twitter a party of one? Is the post about a new and intriguing product being developed by your competitor true? Are your stakeholders as frustrated by your financial projections as one blog suggests? How will you know?

Avoid being misled by following and engaging in multiple social media platforms. A combination of multiple sources of information makes social media valuable. The ability to access the voices of a multiplicity of stakeholders provides you with more confidence in your observations and the impact these observations have on your strategic direction. Though extremely useful, keep in mind that social media is only part of the input you receive. Your interpretations, your valuations, and the conclusions you draw should be influenced by social media. Never allow social media to dictate them. Remember that you are the manager, and social media is your tool. This doesn't work in reverse.

Chapter 10
Metrics and Social Media

"I know half my advertising is wasted,
I just don't know which half."

– John Wanamaker

In 2007, Johnson & Johnson created a Facebook application called the "Acuvue Wink." Like poking someone or sending them a drink, this app allowed users to choose an animated pair of eyes and a message to send to friends. This time, the branding worked. When the campaign was at its peak, 10,000 Facebook users were "winking" every day. Some 65,000 people downloaded the app between the beginning of August and the end of the year. Initially, Johnson & Johnson hoped to reach 100,000 people and achieve half a million winks. In reality, they reached *half a million people* and surpassed *one million winks* (two winks per person). Sales of the 1-Day Acuvue Moist contact lenses increased 17% (Sterne, 2010, p. 43). It would be nice if measuring the impact of social media were always this easy.

Metrics Measurement

Television programs are measured by their Nielson ratings; the higher the ratings, the more programs can charge for advertising. Professional athletes are paid by their statistics. Managers' bonuses are often linked to their company's profits. Customer service reps are evaluated on calls returned, length of calls, and customer satisfaction. College acceptances are based on SAT scores, grade point averages, and recommendations. Loans are given based on credit ratings. Metrics are important in our organizational world; social media metrics are equally important but very different.

Media has always been evaluated for efficacy. Companies demand return on their advertising investment. Someone has to explain why paying $2 million for a 30-second advertisement during the Super Bowl will pay off for a company or brand. (In fact, Pepsi Cola did not advertise in the Super Bowl in 2011. Instead, they invested $20 million in the social media Pepsi Refresh Project.) Measuring returns has always been difficult. Some large packaged goods companies have accurate models that predict that spending $60 million on a certain advertising campaign will gain 1.45% of market share (hypothetical numbers). Most metric management is not as accurate.

A short history of television program evaluation is illustrative. In the 1960s, the Nielson Company sent out viewing logs to selected households. An adult member of the household was supposed to fill out the log with names of the TV programs and who (in the household) was watching them. The household was given gifts or small amounts of money. It became clear that Nielson could not verify who completed the logs or when they were filled out.

In a new approach, Nielson developed a box that, when placed on a television, would tell which channel was on and for how long. Yet they could not verify if anyone was really watching the programs. Then they developed a heat sensory box that would verify if people were actually watching the programs. But they did not factor in whether it was a person or Fido, the incontinent dog. This short history does not mean to poke fun at Nielson—a leading company in media metric management. Instead, this story is used to illustrate how difficult it is to measure the impact of media.

Tensions and Social Media Measurement

Measuring social media impact is a difficult task, complete with several tensions. First, there is tension in the long term versus the short term. We know that quick hits in social media are not very meaningful. Social media conversations, promotions, and initiatives are long-term investments and payoffs. Matt Kucharski, managing director of the public relations firm Padilla Speer Beardsley, said of his organization's blog, "Readership in those first few months was pretty lame—like shouting in an empty parking lot. Slowly but surely, we started getting people to follow our posts, and we started following theirs" (Kucharski, 2010, para. 3). Now they are having ongoing conversations with multiple stakeholders. Social media tools need time to build that momentum.

Second, it is difficult to measure emotion. This is called "sentiment analysis" in social media terminology. Some media metric companies try to measure emotional response by doing key word analysis, but it has its limitations. You can pull the words "Nike" and "pleasure" out of blogs, tweets, and other media 653 times, but is the "pleasure" really about Nike, being with a person who is wearing Nikes, or running in the wilderness? A statement might also be sarcastic. "It is always a pleasure to get blisters from my new Nikes." Nuances are not always picked up by content analyses. Some companies, such as Kane Consulting, actually analyze tweet by tweet in order to correctly interpret meaning and nuance.

Lastly, as in most advertising efforts, the tension of measuring costs is ever-present. You can cost out an ad on Facebook, but you cannot measure the exact impact. Social media efforts build on each other and cannot be seen in isolation. A single customer may see an advertisement for your company on Facebook, have a friend who tweets nicely about your company on Twitter, and also read a blog that positively references your company; all of these things work in harmony to build your brand. So, how does one measure the impact of a conversation? Or, in many cases, how does one measure the cost of having that conversation? Building brand is a long-term proposition; short-term measures do not always work.

Key Questions in Social Media Metrics

In many ways this exploration of metrics is more about questions than answers. Here are some important ones to consider:

- How do you measure engagement in a conversation?
- What is the ROI of your phone?
- What will success look like in your social media endeavors?
- In what time frame will you measure your success?
- Are your expectations for return on social media endeavors irrational?
- Which metrics are most important to your organization?
- How does one measure the depth of positive emotional response for one's customer base (short of tattooing a logo like Harley lovers do)?
- What are the goals for your social media efforts?
- Do you want ROI or impact?

Old System/New System Framework

In many traditional marketing textbooks, metrics were often spelled out with the acronym AIDA—attention, interest, desire, action. These were the levels of success of a promotional piece or campaign. After airing a Super Bowl commercial, for instance, a marketing research company might call 2,000 homes and ask questions related to the commercial. Did you notice a commercial about financial services (attention)? Are you interested in more information about financial services (interest)? Would you like the benefits described by the financial services commercial (desire)? Would you like me to put you in touch with one of the representatives of the company (action)? Based on the results of those questions (based on the AIDA model), the financial services company may get some short-term results of their ads.

More recently, Jim Sterne, author of *Social Media Metrics* (2010), has posited another typology of metrics for social media marketing:

- **Getting Attention:** What is posted about you?

- **Getting Respect:** How often is your message passed on?

- **Getting Emotional:** What words are followers and detractors using?

- **Getting Response:** How many are clicking into your messages?

- **Getting the Message/Hearing the Conversation:** Are the right people hearing the right message?
- **Getting Results:** Are enough people buying? Are your champions pushing your products/services to others?

Besides this framework, Sterne also writes about customer engagement and customer listening levels. How closely are customers listening and responding? Other authors, marketing gurus, and consultants use other frameworks. Essentially, they all come down to awareness, engagement, conversation, action, and referral to others. Can you create champions who will be evangelical about your products/services to others? You cannot accomplish this overnight—it takes steps, trust building, and give-and-take. Creating champions takes a steady stream of social media presence. Still, champions may never tattoo your logo on their cheek.

Best Buy, the large electronics retailer, takes social media and social media metrics seriously. Among other things, it

- knows how much each "fan" on Facebook is worth in terms of investment;
- buys several analytics packages in order to follow tweet mentions, fans, reach, volume of conversion, volume of conversation, influence of social media, number of mentions, and customer engagement;

- created Twelpforce where customers can tweet questions and receive responses 24/7;
- gives key employees the ability to respond on Twitter through Twelpforce to customers and measures employee activity.

For Best Buy, social media is and will remain an important part of its marketing strategy.

Which Metrics?

Once you have been told to develop metrics for your social media efforts, which metrics do you use? The answer is clear: It depends on what you want to accomplish and which social media tools you plan on using. Again, it is difficult to take any given tool in isolation and evaluate it without a larger context and its connecting points to other tools.

If you wish to look at the impact of your tweets, you can count the number of "followers" you have, the number of "re-tweets" (the number of your followers sending your tweet on to their followers—this can be a huge multiplier effect), and the number of times that you are referenced by others. The company Klout will measure how many times your tweet has been re-tweeted. Using Klout, a company can quickly assess the impact of positive or negative commentary. If you wish to go deeper, you can do a content analysis on the references to you and count the number of positive and negative words.

Metrics and Social Media

The analysis of your blog might even be easier. WordPress (and other blog sites) allows you to see the number of people clicking into your blog on a daily basis. You can even see how many of these people are "new" viewers. More importantly, you can see how many people comment on your blog (engage you in conversation). Using Google Analytics, you can gather more detailed information: country of origin, internet connection speed, time of day, and path through your website. For blogs, then, your metrics may include audience growth, conversation rate (visitor comments divided by your posts), and external citations (some kind of ripple index).

The short-term results of Facebook ads are fairly easy to measure. You can count the times someone has clicked through the ad to your website. You can count those who have made a purchase. You can measure the cost of this campaign and the short-term results. You cannot necessarily measure those who see your ad and add a notch to your credibility or those who buy something two years later based on what they read today.

YouTube metrics are simple. How many people have clicked into the video? This number does not measure how many people watched the video in its entirety. It does not measure reaction except the number of viewers who have clicked "like" or "dislike" after (or before) they see the video. You can count the number of people who have put your

YouTube video on their Facebook or LinkedIn account. You can read the comments on your YouTube video as well. In raw numbers, though, the quantity of viewers is a good indication of how viral your YouTube video has gone.

Social media author Brian Solis writes and speaks regularly about "conversion science." Essentially, conversion science is how to convert impressions into action. Conversations, followers, and fans are fine, but are they buying? How do you convert these relationships to cash in the register? Solis writes that you develop your ideal ends—sales, orders, foot traffic, memberships, contributions—and then measure them as if you were a scientist, before and after your social media activities. Sound easy? The problem lies in the beginning and end of these activities. Even if it is not an exact science, organizations must try to measure outcomes; sooner or later, funders will ask for these numbers.

One disturbing recent study by a psychologist Stephen Lewis suggested that the many YouTube videos on cutting and self-injury were glamorizing the practices. These videos have over two million hits. Lewis, an assistant professor at the University of Guelph in Ontario, Canada, suggests that these YouTube videos are influencing other youth to engage in self-injury. Lewis used YouTube metrics to indicate how potent these videos are. He suggested that more YouTube videos against self-injury be created and placed on YouTube.

An interrelated topic is the infamous SEO or "search engine optimization." Google and other search engines display websites and other forms of texts based on algorithms. Consultants can "make sure" that your blog or website or web ad gets good play by using the right words. These words trigger higher ratings when one is "Googled" and make your information more likely to be viewed by clients. A metric would be how high one is in those ratings.

Ultimately, an organization must consider the following metrics: traffic, share of voice, inbound links, new members, new member satisfaction, bounce rate, and brand mention.

> ### Hypothetical ROI Model (Metricsman, 2010)
>
> - **(Data)** Total potential unduplicated reach of the five tweets is 1,000,000 people
> - **(Assume)** 10% of the potential audience will actually see the tweet = 100,000 people
> - **(Assume)** 20% of the individuals who see the tweet find it relevant to them = 20,000 people
> - **(Assume)** 10% of those finding it relevant will visit the site = 2,000 people
> - **(Assume)** 10% of those visiting the site will convert and buy the product = 200 people
> - **(Data)** Incremental profit margin on each sale is $50
> - **(Data)** Total cost of social media initiative is $2,400
>
> **ROI Calculation:** (200 x $50) = $10,000 – $2,400 = $7,600/$2,400 = 3.17 x 100 = 317% ROI

Where to Get Metrics

Some metrics are easily accessible. For instance, a user of WordPress can easily access metrics associated with his or her blog. GoogleRatings and Google Analytics allow users to easily access metrics. These metrics are free but not always in the depth that a user desires. Other companies, such as Telium, Twitrratr, and HubSpot, provide metrics for a fee.

- **Telium:** Telium touts its ability to perform web analytics. It examines web-based communication for mentions of your brand and can ascertain if your website or web tool is receiving an optimal amount of traffic. It will map solutions for optimizing this consumer flow.

- **Twitrratr:** Twitrratr scans Twitter content for mentions of your brand. It classifies words as positive, negative, and neutral, and provides you with a readout of these ratings.

- **HubSpot:** HubSpot is a marketing analytics company. It helps a client analyze and evaluate its marketing efforts. It improves a website's likelihood of being found and provides SEO tools. It can also help you position yourself with your blog and draw more readers.

Many other tools exist. Klout gauges online influence. PostRank Analytics measures many metrics around impressions that your messages are making. This short analysis does not pretend to be a comprehensive view of metric tools and purveyors of market analytics. Nor is the promotion of any aforementioned company intended. What *is* intended is to offer an idea of what is available for those interested in evaluating their social media efforts.

Where to Get Metrics

Social media is a tricky business. It is much like the three men and the elephant. How you describe the elephant will determine how you perceive its value or usefulness to you. Are you trying to build short-term sales or a long-term brand? Are you trying to restore trust? Are you trying to understand customers and potential customers? Are you trying to have hundreds of people read your blog? Do you want 35% of your followers to re-tweet your tweet regularly?

First, social media efforts are a long-term investment. You have to be willing to pay to play. If you expect extreme results in three months, you may be supremely disappointed. Most organizations are in the investment phase rather than the returns phase. Second, your social media efforts are interwoven; typically they do not work in isolation, and you cannot easily evaluate their individual results. Third, if you think you can control the conversation, you are sorely wrong. Social media inter actions about your brand are no longer in your control; you can influence them, but you need to be creative to do so.

Chapter 11
Social Capital: The Deposits and Withdrawals of Social Media

> "If Facebook were a country, it would surpass the United States as the third largest country in the world."
>
> – Qualman, 2010

What Is It?

Every minute, 1,789,736 actions take place on Facebook alone, according to a report in *Time* magazine in December 2010 (Grossman, 2010). Considering the sheer mass of comments, photos, messages, status updates, and shared links, it is easy to see why organizations are realizing that if their stakeholders (employees, customers, potential customers, and competitors) are already engaged, they might want to get in on the action. Managers need to begin this engagement process, the currency of which is social capital.

Social media requires an investment just like any other business transaction. There is even a capital investment structure much like financial or economic capital. In financial terms, capital is money used to create or buy goods or services in order to sell them again. There is a process of exchange. An investment and an exchange are required in order to be successful in social media. You can't withdraw the benefits if you haven't invested upfront. By this point, you should be recognizing some of the many benefits you'd like to withdraw. Now it is time to start developing your capital structure and investing. However, here is where you don't want to be naïve. There is more to investing in social media than just the time you spend online or the money you spend on consultants who can get you up and running and pointed in the right direction.

Social media has a capital structure all its own, frequently referred to as social capital. In *The Whuffie Factor: Using the Power of Social Networks to Build Your Business,* a seminal work on social media, author Tara Hunt (2009) popularizes the term *whuffie* for social capital, terminology she appropriated from Cory Doctorow's *Down and Out in the Magic Kingdom* (2003). In this book, social capital is referred to in terms of exchanges, in recognition of the intrinsic nature of this reciprocity. This give-and-take is essential to the social capital structure and intricately connected (I share something with you and you *use* that something to create something you will then share with me). No matter what you call it, consider social capital the significant contribution you add to the collective body of knowledge on your social media site(s) and all the sites that interact with yours. You need to add "stuff" that co-mingles with other "stuff" to create new awareness from which you can withdraw new information or insights you might have otherwise missed. Don't worry: examples and specifics follow.

How Do You Create It?

Thinking about social capital requires looking at social media engagement like the proverbial three-legged stool. One leg is the audience with whom you want to connect. The second leg is your objective for engagement—that is, what do I hope to get out of this? The final leg is what "stuff" you have to share. These three "legs" have to be internally consistent. It won't make sense to share good stuff with the wrong audience. Likewise, you won't want to create a dialogue that doesn't provide continuing interest for you. Just like you can't put one leg on a stool and try it out (you have to put on all three legs to make sure it works), you need to consider all three facets of social capital. Thus, ask yourself the following nonlinear yet interrelated questions:

With whom do I want to connect?
(customers, potential market segment, competitors, etc.)

Why am I engaging?
(looking for new customers, looking for "on-the-street" opinions, reinforcing brand, etc.)

What can I share?
(links to interesting content in our field, engaging stories about our organization, thought-provoking questions, humor, etc.)

Note that you might have more than one answer to these questions, and that's great. Just like your financial portfolios, you should be diversified in social capital.

You're almost ready to start investing in the social capital market, but you need to use the answers you just identified to determine where your investments will go. Where will you make your deposits and withdrawals? In previous chapters, we have identified a wide variety of social media opportunities. Align your three legs to the social media strategies and objectives that suit your needs, then get started.

As you think about creating social capital for investment, consider Acker and Smith's (2010) characteristics of highly engaging social media campaigns. These nine characteristics are essential to successful campaigns because they embody the key elements of healthy social capital.

- **Transparency:** See our detailed discussion of this characteristic in Chapter 3.
- **Interactivity between Stakeholders:** Connect the various participants for shared insights between customers or clients, suppliers, management, and employees.
- **Immediacy:** Share information "in the moment" for authenticity rather than "after the fact" when history can rewrite itself.
- **Facilitation:** Rather than controlling information, take care to coordinate the sharing of real information, even if it is conflicting.
- **Commitment:** Create an environment where this comes from all the stakeholders for the good of all the stakeholders.
- **Co-creation:** Both ideas and ways to implement them come from the various stakeholders.
- **Collaboration:** Goals are transparent and there is commitment to work together to achieve them.
- **Experience:** The bottom line is not only revenue but the experiences of the consumers.
- **Trust:** All the stakeholders believe in the commitment and authenticity of the others.

Pull it all together! Aligning the considerations of your three-legged stool and incorporating as many of these nine characteristics as you can will allow you to begin building your social capital. Remember that this is a dynamic process, and you need to watch for change that will impact the nine characteristics and how you deploy them. Because you are dealing with people and dynamic situations, you need to be agile in your response to changes. Consider the following great example of response agility: At the 2008 Blackboard BbWorld conference, attendees flooded Twitter with complaints about minimal wireless accessibility. Within hours (agility!), a ballroom was opened with unlimited wireless access.

What Does It Look Like?

Paula Werne is the director of public relations for Holiday World & Splashin' Safari, a family-owned theme and water park in Santa Claus, Indiana. She is a social media exemplar and is often invited to share her experiences at industry gatherings. *FUNWORLD* magazine profiled her as a "Creative Communicator" in 2007. As of 2011, readers can explore Paula's presence on Facebook, Twitter, Holiblog (the company blog), CoasterBuzz (an enthusiasts' club and newsletter), Theme Park Review (another enthusiasts' club and newsletter), and ultimaterollercoaster.com (an enthusiasts' website). She also creates YouTube and Flickr collections of Holiday World videos and photos and contributes to related sites like *Budget Travel* when the topics align with Holiday World. Paula was an early social media adopter, so her expertise (and her social capital deposits and withdrawals) have grown organically over the years she has invested in social media. This is important to note, because social media continues to be a dynamic evolving opportunity, so the philosophy of organically cultivating your social capital is as important as the technology. The technology will continue to evolve, along with the ways people use it.

Back in 2005, Paula had zero engagement in social media. The theme park had added a new roller coaster and themed area, and Paula was looking for a way to share her enthusiasm and the information she had previously only been able to disseminate in press releases and press visits to the park. She decided to try a blog, and Holiblog was born. As Twitter, Facebook, and MySpace were taking off, Paula had to decide where she could get the best return for the time investment in social media she was willing to make. The choices she made were less analytical and more a gut-feel about where she could best reach her potential audience. She chose Twitter for quick snippets of connections and CoasterBuzz to connect to a specific industry enthusiast community. Her most difficult choice was between Facebook and MySpace, but she chose Facebook because her instincts told her that she would find more engagement. Her hunch proved correct, and she now has a broad following of over 150,000 Facebook friends who "like" this site and constantly interact with a diverse community.

That was over 10 years ago, and Paula has found a great return on investment in these social media sites. She has grown her audience to include hardcore fans, potential visitors, and industry leaders. In addition to communicating news about new rides and other park information, a stated goal is to demonstrate the family values aspect of the park to the outside world. Paula wants her listeners to know and identify with the Koch family who owns and operates the park and their values of fun, friendliness, cleanliness, and family togetherness. She also fosters a dialogue with her fans and "friends" that contributes to her company's understanding of its market and potential.

What kinds of things does Paula share? On Twitter, she might provide a quick link to a YouTube video about the park or to industry news. She comments on CoasterBuzz about happenings in Holiday World. On Facebook, she engages in personal conversations with those who follow her. On a typical week, she might ask for ideas for new items in the gift shops or in the restaurants. She asks friends to support Holiday World by voting for their park or rides in fan polls. She runs contests about old-time photos that remind her followers about the longevity and family-based traditions of the organization. She provides real information on job fairs, open employment positions, and new employees. She posts pictures of new construction and scenes from the park, even in the winter when the park is closed. Recently she ran a contest asking friends to name a new park ride. She advertised a TV show that highlighted a new Holiday World water ride and beloved roller coaster. She runs videos showcasing the park president and his mom (the company matriarch) to personally connect her viewers with the family owners.

What Happens When Social Capital Gets Unpredictable?

It's not difficult to understand how—with all this authenticity, transparency, and connection between a wide variety of stakeholders—social capital can be slippery to control. You are dealing with people here: people who connect to you but people over whom you have little direct influence. Many entities contribute to your social capital, and sometimes your best planning can go awry. Consider the following three stories of unpredictable social capital:

Story 1

Jason Fried (2011) describes the situation his company, 37signals, navigated when one of its key products, Campfire, malfunctioned. Campfire is a real-time chat tool used by thousands of businesses. These businesses were rightfully frustrated when the software went down for as long as 45 minutes at a time. These companies vented on

Twitter publicly and explicitly. Fried and his partner, David Heinemeier Hansson, recognized the need to be honest and transparent. This was not the time to hide behind excuses or formalities. Instead, they

- posted updates on the company's website;
- shared the process;
- shared results;
- shared the things they still didn't understand;
- responded to angry tweets on Twitter one at a time.

The Twitter responses were the most personal. Hansson's statements included comments like: "We're battling demons on all fronts and losing. It's pathetic, I know." And "We're spending the goodwill we've built from years of reliable service like it's going out of style." And (our favorite): "You can only say duh! so many times before people just think you're annoying. We're way past that." Their customers more than appreciated their authenticity and transparency, and responses were positive, "Way to go on being awesome and communicative to your customers," "37signals has been giving a free lesson in customer service and honesty the past few weeks." This frustrating malfunction turned into an outstanding opportunity to manage unpredictability and actually *grow* social capital in the process.

Story 2

In the summer of 2010, Steven Slater gained fame as the Jet Blue flight attendant who deplaned down an emergency slide after a hostile verbal encounter with a passenger. In a tough economic environment, he became a folk hero to thousands of frustrated workers. As of 2011, there are 10 Facebook pages devoted to the disgruntled Jet Blue employee. *Free Steven Slater* has the largest following with almost 33,000 fans. This self-organizing support went viral as workers debated Slater's actions in relationship to his employer's expectations, his responsibilities, his courage, and his consequences. This underscores the unpredictability of social capital. Jet Blue certainly hadn't planned this event in their social media campaign strategies. It is interesting to note that Jet Blue stayed out of the discussions. Although Jet Blue has a reputation for ongoing and dynamic interaction in various social media venues, they were silent here. Whether they were avoiding the discussion because of possible legal action or they simply had nothing to add to the conversation, they let this engagement develop without them. Sometimes social capital is best developed by knowing when *not* to take part in the conversation.

Story 3

In 2009, Honda decided to introduce its upcoming Crosstour CUV on a Facebook page. Fans contributed many negative opinions about the look of the new vehicle. Very positive comments appeared from a contributor named Eddie, who was subsequently identified by other fans as the product manager. In his post, Eddie did not identify himself as the product manager nor even as a Honda employee. This frustrated Facebook fans even more and generated much negative publicity for Honda. Honda removed Eddie's posts (they said) because he neither identified himself as an employee nor was a company spokesperson. Honda, in addition, issued a press release defending the car, explaining Eddie, and thanking fans for "all of their interest." This example has been identified on multiple websites as a "social media disaster" (Barros, 2009): lack of transparency, lack of authenticity, and limited real connection to fans even in the apology release.

How do you monitor your social capital in order to recognize both the predictable and unpredictable opportunities? First, you need to be constantly engaged in the give-and-take of your social capital. There is an initial cost: research, time, and creativity commensurate with your organization and message. You need to participate by actively monitoring your social media sites. You need to interact as a consistent, dependable presence. You need to **be**

there! Be on the lookout for those with whom you will connect and who will connect with you (they are not always your customers).

In addition to your own engagement, there are a variety of Web-based and software applications that can help. This list is growing every day, but here are some current applications to get you thinking and started.

- Google Alerts is a free application that emails you when a specific phrase or word you identify is used online. (Paula from Holiday World uses this one for the name of the park, specific people, and industry terms.)

- Twilerts, also free, sends regular email updates of Twitter tweets that contain any keyword you identify. Useful keywords might be your brand, product, service, or organization name.

- Yext Rep identifies reviews and/or mentions of your organization on social media websites and is also free.

- Viralheat follows and reports online discussions by geographical area. This application charges a monthly fee.

- Trackur monitors keyword use in blogs and articles. After a free trial, there is a monthly fee.

Tying It All Together

Social capital is at once simple (it's just communication, after all) and complex (it involves dynamic and unpredictable individuals). Independent of your own engagement, it's happening all around you, and your competitors are actively investing and withdrawing. As you (a manager) consider your organization's social capital potential, consider these final thoughts and tips from Paula Werne at Holiday World.

> **Paula's Thoughts and Tips**
>
> - Social capital is "word of mouth on steroids."
> - Social capital is not an ad; it's an ongoing conversation.
> - Investing in social capital behavior is like going to a party; you have to understand what is appropriate and the ways you are expected to act and interact. Know the cultural norms.
> - Social capital hasn't replaced our old communications strategies like press kits and news releases. You have to do it all.
> - Social media gives you the opportunity to demonstrate that there is nothing to hide. This is the truth. This keeps your communications real.

Social Capital

- Before you start, ask yourself these questions: What is the brand? What is the story?
- Strategize at the beginning about how you want your social capital to "feel." For Holiday World, the strategy is feeling like family. Paula's social capital is designed to "feel like a letter from home."
- Be yourself, but "not so much of yourself that you go off base" and lose the brand, story, or "feeling" of your organization.
- Holiday World doesn't use metrics to track value ("there's not a magic formula"). Paula's measure is fan numbers and "friend" numbers increasing. "We don't look for hard return on investment."
- Remember that even though we use technology, this is **not** technical. "It's just communicating!"
- Complaints make social media engagement more real. "Swallow hard—sometimes it's not fair."
- Sometimes you will be compelled to respond to criticism or incorrect information for sake of accuracy. Try patience first. Social media works best if your fans and followers self-regulate your message for you.

- If you feel that you have to respond to missing or inaccurate information, "weigh the pros and cons. Think about who's looking."
- The time investment is significant.
- This is fun!

Chapter 12
The Ethics of Social Media

Fact or Fiction

Several years ago, Oprah Winfrey promoted an author who had falsified parts of his memoir. When she discovered the truth, she admonished him on her program. She drew the line between fact and fiction. Most publishers, as well as journalists, in the past, checked out the veracity of what they published. This was the implicit contract between the author and publishing industry, and the reader.

With social media, anyone can literally publish anything anytime. The line between fact and opinion becomes blurred as a blog is one's "blog," a daily or weekly rumination, and a combination of fact and fiction. YouTube videos about an organization may have been created by that organization, or maybe not. Whether created by the organization or not, it may be an embellishment or a downright untruth. People "dis" each other all the time in Facebook with opinions and half-facts.

Blurred Lines

Clearly, social media sites have blurred even further the line between fact and fiction. The ethics of responsibility have shifted from the author to the reader. The reader *has* to be more critically engaged in the discernment of truth because the author does not have to be.

Introduction

Like any new technology or field, the ethics of social media is growing, morphing, and contentious. One person's excellent marketing research practice is another person's violation of privacy. One person's deceptive advertising is another person "just putting their best foot forward." Some have decried social networks as traps that will provide big government and big business with all of your private information in order to control and manipulate you. Others have posited that social networks are the great levelers, bound to create true democratization and a free marketplace. The truth lies somewhere in between. This chapter does not answer ethical questions definitively. Rather, it raises some important ones and attempts to examine them from several angles.

Public Space

Social media is public space. In that way, it can be likened to a public park. All sorts of people can use it in a variety of ways: competing in kickball, necking with a lover, strolling with a friend, playing hide-and-seek, taking illegal drugs, writing memos on a computer, reading a novel, or picnicking with your family and friends. People use parks to connect with nature, themselves, and their friends; it can be an aesthetic, spiritual, intellectual, or social experience.

Like the park goers who use the park for their own unique activities, social networks are used in a large variety of ways. Facebook's 500 million participants all use the site differently. Most online social networkers use this media to improve their social, intellectual, aesthetic, spiritual, or business lives. But like parks, social networks have their lurkers, muggers, thieves, and occasional murderers. Some abuse these public spaces for their own gains at the expense of others. No set of ethics will impede their actions, but for the rest of us, it is valuable to look at the ethics of social media and its use in the workplace.

The Study of Ethics

What we call "ethics" is essentially a set of guiding moral principles. Many ethical frameworks are timeless and can therefore be applied to current issues. Consequential ethics deals with the consequences of ethics—making choices by optimizing the end results, regardless of the rightness or wrongness of the original actions. So, it might be okay to steal from a crook if you donate the money to a good cause. On the other hand, normative ethics deals with making choices based on what is right in the first place, regardless of the consequences. So, you shouldn't really steal from a crook. Utilitarian ethics posits that the best course of action is the one that will provide the most benefit for the most people. So, if you steal millions from the Lord in the manor and give it to peasants for food, this is an okay practice. Buddha, Jesus, Confucius, Aristotle, Plato, and others have put forth their own codes and principles of ethics over the past several thousand years.

Though the study of ethics is not new, it has undergone increased examination at some of the high profile business events of the past 20 years. The predicaments of Enron, WorldCom, and other large companies that have failed have brought the subject of ethics to the forefront of conversation. The rise and fall of Bernie Madoff and the subsequent loss of the fortunes of individuals and organizations have also helped bring this subject into the limelight. Other highly publicized ethics issues include huge oil profits, deceptive advertising, and executive salaries.

It has been argued that it is difficult to uphold a single set of ethical principles in a pluralistic society like the one in which we currently live. Too many kinds of people, with divergent value sets, think in too many different ways. Yet there are always guidelines for behaving ethically in a situation. Perhaps an ethical litmus test might be, "If your actions were published on the front page of the newspaper, would you be okay with your parents and grandparents reading about it? If not, why?" If you are not comfortable with your actions being scrutinized by those whose respect you desire, then you might wish to re-evaluate your actions.

> **Some Common Ethical Imperatives**
>
> - **Honesty:** Always tell the truth.
> - **Transparency:** Always be forward about your intentions.
> - **Respect:** Always hold the "other" in highest regard.
> - **Privacy:** Allow the "other" to share only what they are willing.
> - **Responsibility:** Take ownership of your actions.

Central Ethical Issues

Privacy

The central ethical issue in social media is privacy. How can I ensure that the information that I share is safe and not shared with corporations or unsavory characters? Quite frankly, you cannot. If you put a sign up in a public park that you are blond, six-foot-one, educated at Montana State, married to Brianna, work at Walmart, and like Bono, *anyone*, and I do mean *anyone*, can write down that information and run with it. You can never really know how that information is used. Some sixteen-year-olds in Uzbekistan might sell it to Chechen poppy dealers, for all you know.

For the rest of us, if we are trying to play nicely in the park and desire to continue to do so in the future, we have to respect the privacy of others. If we say that we are going to keep information private, we need to follow through with our commitment. If we betray our commitment to the privacy of others, given the transparency of social media, we will be eviscerated by our constituencies. We might do some damage, and that damage will ultimately bring us down.

Recently, the alumni department of a Midwestern college was faced with a privacy dilemma. Many of their alumni had "fanned" the school's alumni Facebook page, indicating that they were fans of the college. Although they had "fanned" the institution, countless alumni had not provided their emails (used for fundraising) to the alumni office. Could the college now use its Facebook links to these individuals to garner their emails, which would be used in fundraising? Would this be a violation of the privacy of the alumni "fans"?

This ethical issue slides over into the legal arena—especially with credit card and other financial information. There are strict laws bounding the issue. The ethics get fuzzy when financial data is hacked. Is the company who was hacked ethically responsible because they did not invest enough money in firewalls? Maybe so. What if the records of a university, hospital, or psychiatrist are hacked?

To what extent are entities ethically responsible if they have taken the appropriate precautions to render confidential information safe?

Another grey area when examining privacy in social media is the potential "harm to reputation." (This too could slide over to the legal realm.) If you share a piece of information—whether about a drunken escapade, the use of anti-depression meds, or a past abortion—where does the ethical responsibility reside? Does the blame rest on your shoulders because you shared information with an unreliable source? Did the person who shared your information violate any previously established promises or commitments concerning that information? What if there was no commitment, just common decency?

The flip side of privacy emerged recently with a "tweet" sent out by an employee of a media agency representing Chrysler Corporation. He sent out what he thought was a private tweet about the f****** drivers in Detroit. It was in his public account and before he could recall it, the message was retweeted and became part of the public domain. Whoops. Apparently, he was fired. Careful what you share—it may become public domain.

Honesty of Identity

We explored the issue of authenticity in an earlier chapter. The central question, "Are you who you say you are?" becomes literal in the exploration of ethics. Are you writing the blog or is a team of writers doing it for you? Are you answering your tweets or is a staff member? Executives and politicians have ghost writers; that is part of their game. Part of the implicit contract of listening to a public speaker of that caliber is the cognizance that they did not write their own material. So where is the appropriate dividing line between being disingenuous or deceptive and being honest with your readers?

Employer/Employee Relationships

Social networks are public parks. Because of this, they can be used by *everyone*. Can an employer sniff around social media sites to learn more about an applicant or current employee? Absolutely—and many of them do. Whatever a person writes on these sites is open for the public. Yet, does that mean it is "public"?

Clearly, organizations believe that social media sites are open for scrutiny and input for hiring/retaining practices. Domino's Pizza fired two employees for producing a disgusting YouTube video. A Midwestern university announced that it had not accepted applicants because of the contents of their social media accounts. A nonprofit organization fired an employee for the contents of his Facebook account because it "did not fit with the mission of the organization." One large electronics company fired an employee because he partook in a

The Ethics of Social Media

blog against that company. Even the great Green Bay turned Minnesota Viking quarterback Brett Favre was fined by the National Football League for his alleged "sexting" to a media correspondent.

Back in the 1980s, I was a candidate for a manager position at General Electric. GE hired a consultant to follow up with every stage of my resume. The consultant called (this was before email) all of the people I had worked for and even a professor or two. In the end, I didn't get the job. I did, however, have the opportunity to read the comprehensive report the consultant had compiled that was scarily accurate in its detailed explanation of why I was deemed a poor long-term fit for the position at GE. I was very impressed and thankful to the consultant who had saved me from accepting the wrong job. What I took away from this report, and most important to our topic, was the way the consultant had used all of the information available to create a profile of me. The same process is still used and considered ethical today, only now companies often turn to social media for resources.

While individuals might see their social network communication as a private affair, employers obviously do not always agree. In this case, perhaps ethics do not matter. These cases are similar to whispering a secret to a best buddy on a playground, yes, again in a park. Your friend agrees never to tell a soul, and yet they do. You get burned, but have learned a valuable lesson. Better not write anything on a blog, Facebook, or Twitter that you would not want your Human Resource Department, potential college admissions board, sorority sisters, or grandmother to read.

Deception

The ethics of deception for social media is similar to any other situation. It is never nice to be deceptive. The common defense of deception is the pathetic vulnerability of the masses. You've heard the common vendor phrase, "a sucker is born every second." There have even been cases in Minnesota and Massachusetts of predators on craigslist luring unsuspecting victims to lonely spots and murdering them. Many people have been burned buying something on craigslist or eBay because what was advertised was not what was delivered.

A friend bought a motor scooter on eBay that was advertised having 3,000 miles on it. Once he returned home, he was surprised to discover, needless to say, that it actually had 33,000 miles on it! He was forced to take the sellers to court to recoup his investment. Craigslist has no real recourse for these situations. eBay, on the other hand, maintains a blacklist of unsavory users. On dating sites, the issues are similar. You submit your weight, salary, and age. Certainly, these figures are often fudged to make profiles more appealing.

Society tells us not to lie and to "do no harm." But in reality, we are living in a world where not everyone plays by those rules. Therefore, buyer: beware.

Boundaries/Friending

Yes, we know that "friend" is really a noun and not a verb, but, thanks to Facebook, the English language is being redefined once again. Who can you friend? Who can't you friend? Many children do not want to be "friends" with their parents; they want Facebook to be their private playground. You can be friends with anyone you want… or can you?

As a professor, I have often discussed the issue. Because I maintain a power relationship with my students—power over the grade—I do not have the ethical right to "friend" my students. This is because they might feel obliged to say "yes" even if they do not want to do so. The private business of my students is not my business, unless they open it up to me. This would be true for any "power" relationship: boss/secretary, therapist/client, or employer/employee.

Corporations are now setting policies for employee involvement in social media. How and what an employee can communicate on organizational social media websites is being limited. Many employees see this as an infringement of their free speech rights. Is this fair? I'm not sure. Think of life before social media. If a company was in the news, say, for an oil spill or an ethical violation, employees were told not to speak with the press. All relationships with the media were conducted by the public relations department. The organization spoke with one solitary voice. Today, a company still aims to respond with one voice and message, and this desire extends to the reach of social media. All other voices heard online are potential distractions and inaccuracies.

Greater Good

Ethics concerns the greater good of the majority. The greater good should be the litmus test of social media behaviors and actions. Does social media serve this purpose? Some say "no." The Chinese government, as well as other governments, decided that Facebook did not serve the greater good of its 1.4 billion people. My own daughter once had an extended stay at a local hospital where she found that Facebook and other social media sites were blocked. Apparently, some of the hospital personnel had been spending too much time online and not enough time with patients, and the hospital blocked access in reaction. Multitudes of organizations have decried that too much employee time is spent on Facebook, reducing productivity significantly.

Social media sites have been said to be responsible (probably accurately) for reduced productivity, unresponsive employees, car accidents, murders, thefts, and breeches of security. On the other hand, social media has become a powerful connector of people, a file-sharing device, a marketing tool, and a brand developer. Each organization has to look at the balance independently, weighing the costs and benefits.

One interesting case in the debate over social media involved a Facebook page formed around the topic of breast feeding. The page helped connect mothers without enough milk with mothers with surplus milk. For the baby nursing community, this site was a godsend. Regardless of the page's usefulness, Facebook blocked it because it contained photographs of naked breasts. Facebook, in its ethical deliberations, does not allow any pictures with perceived pornographic content (bless their dear souls). Yet, access to this site was clearly in the greater public good. Luckily, the two organizations were able to work through the issue amicably.

Conclusion

In 2009, a blogger in the upper Midwest posted a story about a community organizer and his connection in a mortgage fraud. The organizer was fired from his job and sued the blogger. He won a $60,000 settlement. It is being appealed. This is not a new issue: defamation of character versus publication of a version of the truth. What does a "journalist" owe to his/her constituency? What is new is the format and because everyone, and we do mean everyone (120 million strong), can be a blogger and can have strong opinions about an issue or a person, many more cases like this may emerge. Social media can amplify a voice, a message; it can also amplify a controversial message.

Although ethics has always been part of human behavior, the widespread use of social media tools has created new ethical dilemmas. Specifically, the boundaries between privacy and authenticity have been ruffled. Social media sites can lower one's privacy, but they also force one to be authentic. This is because inauthentic behavior is often quickly exposed. YouTube videos go viral in a matter of minutes, exposing that a company's practices do not live up to customer expectations. Egregious behaviors, as noted in the Domino's or United Airlines examples, are brought to light and damage reputations.

Every organization must match its use of social media tools with its own mission, vision, and values. Does its use of social media match its espoused principles? Do all of its employees understand its mission and vision and how they align with social media practices? If not, organizations may end up scrambling to understand social media as a means of damage control.

Chapter 13
The Future of Social Media

Civil War Trip

Say you are in Washington, D.C., for a conference. Say you have four days off and want a mini vacation visiting Civil War battlefields. Say you like high-quality Italian restaurants, like to stay at Marriott Courtyards, and want a day of pampering and toenail painting at a relaxing spa. Oh, and say you have $1,200 to spend. You can leave Washington on Sunday noon, at the close of the conference, and you have a flight out on Thursday night. Today, you would have several strains of interlocking research to do in order to design the perfect trip. In the next rendition of social media, the computer will do that research and send you back several possible itineraries, complete with prices. It will also make the reservations for you.

The Future

Social media, also termed Web 2.0, is about connecting people. Social media, as you have seen, is user-generated content, blogs, videos, photos, and music available to everyone, from your aging grandma in Albuquerque to Al Qaeda militants hidden in an Afghan cave. With social media, everyone can be a rock star, an author, or a filmmaker. Your 8-year-old daughter's blog is read and commented, on, by a 10-year-old girl outside Istanbul, or, sadly, leered over by a 43-year-old, slimy lecher in New Jersey. With social media, these blogs, communications, or videos are embedded into a context like Twitter, Facebook, or YouTube. The individual is the context within the future of social media. Every interaction you make will enter your digital lifestream.

Moreover, the new social media, or Web 3.0, is a repository for information about the individual, for better or worse. The person becomes the context and many, if not all, of the transactions, purchases, websites visited, and music listened to are part of his or her profile. This information will steer other information, specials, and websites toward that individual. So, I might want a high-quality silk lavender shirt, say between $60 and $80. The web has my measurements and shoots me pictures of three different shirts that might work. The shirts are on a 3D picture of me, and I can choose and quickly buy the one that is most appealing.

The next generation of social media is more about context than content. The context of the content is defined by the data stored under a person or an organization. For instance, right now, if I type in "apple," the computer does not know if I am referring to a delicious edible fruit or a computer. If I type in U2, am I interested in a historical event or a musical group? In the future, an application will scan the context of my unique internet profile and decide. This is a web capable of content and context. The web becomes a giant interconnected, easily accessible database rather than a book. It will deliver the right message to the right person at the right time with the right device. This new web adds meaning to data, creating intelligent, reason-driven searches.

The two key terms associated with this form of the web are "semantic web" and "ontology." The semantic web allows the digital collection of you and your activities. It enables an intelligent search of the personalized you. The semantic web makes you the center of searches and creates richer and more relevant searches for you. Ontology is defined as relationships between terms of knowledge. This new web connects contextualized data and makes it usable and valuable.

Caveats

This new meadow of social media is not without its prairie dog holes, manure piles, and thorny thistles. Let us examine them:

- **Privacy:** First and foremost is the "privacy" thing. Who has access to my data? General Mills, Libyan rebels, sex offenders, identity thieves, my mom? This is a real concern, and this issue has not been, and will not be, put to rest soon. Anyone who enters data on computers is at risk. Period. Where there is a mean person, there is a will and a way. Be careful.

- **Digital Divide:** As social media tools become more sophisticated, "haves" will maintain a competitive advantage in society over "have nots." That division will only grow.
- **Addiction:** As virtual gaming becomes more exciting and "smart," it may lead to more addiction among those gamers. Gamers will have a harder time pulling away from their entertainment and take them away from other, perhaps more productive, activities.
- **Forgetting:** As the web becomes capable of doing more, will humans lose their ability to do some of those tasks? Already, because young people have been raised with spell check, their ability to spell has fallen. Will Web 3.0 write papers for students, and then these students fail to learn how to think critically, write concisely, and express their ideas usefully?

We have shown that social media has a downside: time frittered away, privacy impingements, and theft possibilities. With the next version of social media, these issues will even be more accentuated.

The challenge, then, will be to navigate these downsides while at the same time leveraging the contextualized, valuable, and useful connections that social media of the future provides. If there is one thing you have learned through the stories and ideas in this book, we hope it is the dynamic evolution of human connection that has led us to the social media opportunities that exist today. We are confident that collectively we will in the future both influence and navigate this dynamic process. You, as a manager, will also both benefit from social media and shape it. Enjoy the ride!

Final Tweets

We summarize here this book's significant concepts of social media as they relate to you, a manager. As a nod to our microblogging friends who manage and use Twitter, we have limited our bullet points to the requisite 140 characters or less.

- Social media is just the next piece of communication evolution.
- Social media is a group of tools that facilitate conversations.
- Social media facilitates a multiple of exchanges.
- Social media can be unpredictable: be transparent, authentic, and agile!
- Social media creates opportunities for real-time, as-needed information sharing.
- Blogs, Facebook, Twitter can create fans; fans create sales.
- Social media tools should be integrated into larger marketing plan.
- Social media is an innovation; social media tools can facilitate innovative thinking.
- Creating innovations necessitates deep customer understanding; social media can aid this.
- Social media creates partnerships that are fluid, based on need.

- Social media can be instrumental for job searching, recruitment, and retention, because "fit" can be identified.
- When planning strategy, social media allows you to collect data from a "team" that you can dynamically change, based on need.
- Social media is measurable and immeasurable.
- How do you measure the ROI of your cell phone or a deep conversation?
- Retweets, followers, friends, fans, and comments can all be read and analyzed. What do you want?
- Social media has currency: social capital, which requires exchanges of information between you and your connections.
- When creating social capital in social media, ask: With whom do you connect? Why? What information will you create and share?
- What is private? How do you know?
- Social media is immediate, dynamic, and evolving. Use it!

References and Websites

Acker, J., & Smith, A. (2010). *The dragonfly effect: Quick, effective, and powerful ways to use social media to drive social change.* San Francisco, CA: Jossey-Bass.

AllBusiness. (2006, July/August). Aligning communication with company culture at Pitney Bowes. [Web blog post]. Retrieved from http://www.allbusiness.com/operations/facilities-office-equipment/4103318-1.html

Barros, S. (2009). 5 social media disasters. [Web blog post]. Retrieved from http://www.penn-olson.com/2009/09/21/5-social-media-disasters/

Baumann, P. (2011, January 6). Your Facebook is a one-way mirror. [Web blog post]. Retrieved from http://healthissocial.com/facebook/your-facebook-is-a-one-way-mirror/

Career Development. (2011). Networking. [Harvard Business School Alumni online newsletter article]. Retrieved from http://www.alumni.hbs.edu/careers/networking.html

Cohen, J. (2011). B2B Social media example: GE MarkNet. [Web blog post]. Retrieved from http://socialmediab2b.com/2011/02/b2b-social-media-example-ge-marknet/

Davis, L. (2008, October 2). Social media for business—Who's doing it well and how. [Web blog post]. Retrieved from http://www.readwriteweb.com/archives/social_media_for_business_who_is_doing.php

Doctorow, C. (2003). *Down and out in the Magic Kingdom.* New York: Tor.

Fried, J. (2011, Feb 1). How to turn disaster into gold. *Inc. 33*(1), 37–39.

Godin, S. (1999). *Permission marketing: Turning strangers into friends and friends into customers.* New York: Simon & Schuster.

Grossman, L. (2010). Person of the year: Mark Zuckerberg. *Time, 176*(26), 43–75.

Hanson, A. (2010, September 17). 3 B2B social media cases and why they work. [Web blog post]. Retrieved from http://www.arikhanson.com/2010/09/17/3-b2b-social-media-case-studies-and-why-they-work/

Haugen, D. (2009, April). Welcome to Blue Shirt Nation. [*Twin Cities Business* online e-newsletter article]. Retrieved from http://www.tcbmag.com/peoplecompanies/companies/115772p1.aspx

Heine, C. (2011, February 9). Here's the beef: Taco Bell uses lawsuit to lift 'Likes.' [Web blog post]. Retrieved from http://www.clickz.com/clickz/

news/2025408/heres-beef-taco-bell-lawsuit-lift-likes?utm_source=feedburner& utm_medium=feed&utm_campaign=Feed:+clickz+(ClickZ+-+News

Hibbard, C. (2010, February 2). How IBM uses social media to spur employee innovation. [*Social Media Examiner* newsletter article]. Retrieved from http://www.socialmediaexaminer.com/how-ibm-uses-social-media-to-spur-employee-innovation/

Hibbard, C. (2011, March 23). How social media generated $300,000 in software sales in a weekend. [*Social Media Examiner* newsletter article]. Retrieved from http://www.socialmediaexaminer.com/how-social-media-generated-300000-in-software-sales-in-a-weekend/

Hunt, T. (2009). *The whuffie factor: Using the power of social networks to build your business.* New York: Crown Business.

http://www.caringbridge.org/

http://www.ideastorm.com

http://mystarbucksidea.force.com

http://www.startribune.com/local/53049377.html

http://twitter.com/mndottraffic

http://twitter.zappos.com

http://www.youtube.com/user/DeloitteFilmFest

IBMers' blogs. (n.d.). [Web blog post]. Retrieved from http://www.ibm.com/blogs/zz/en/

Kim, W., & Mauborgne, R. (2005). *Blue ocean strategy: How to create uncontested market space and make competition irrelevant.* Boston: Harvard Business Press.

Kucharski, M. (2010, September 17). 5-year anniversary of Padilla's blog—Where's the cake? [Web blog post]. Retrieved from http://www.psbblog.com/archives/2010/09/5year_anniversa.html

Landry, A. (2007, December 9). Punch Pizza, Highland Park, Saint Paul, MN [Web blog post]. Retrieved from http://s4xton.com/1641/punch-pizza-highland-park-saint-paul-mn/

Li, C., & Bernoff, J. (2008). *Groundswell: Winning in a world transformed by social technologies.* Boston: Forrester Research, Inc.

Marqui. (2010, July 22). Authenticity and transparency in social media: Getting it right [Web blog post]. Retrieved from http://www.marqui.com/blog/authenticity-and-transparency-in-social-media-getting-it-right.aspx

Mehrmann, J. (2011). In memory of Circuit City stores. [Web blog post]. Retrieved from http://www.businessknowhow.com/manage/circuitcity.htm

META Group finds more organizations using internal communications to improve employee morale. (2004, June 15). *Business Wire.* [News Release]. Retrieved from http://www.businesswire.com/news/home/20040615005032/en/CORRECTING-REPLACING-META-Group-Finds-Organizations-Internal

Metricsman. (2010, December 30). Social media measurement 2011: Five things to forget and five things to learn. [Web blog post]. Retrieved from http://metricsman.wordpress.com/

Morrison, M. (2011, January 25). Taco Bell sued for bogus beef. [Web blog post]. Retrieved from http://adage.com/adages/post?article_id=148481

Pentland, A. (2009). How social networks network best. [*HBR List 2009* online newsletter]. Retrieved from http://hbr.org/web/2009/hbr-list/how-social-networks-work-best

Qualman, E. (2010, May 5). Social media revolution video (refreshed). {Web blog video]. Retrieved from http://www.socialnomics.net/2010/05/05/social-media-revolution-2-refresh/

Schawbel, D. (2009, February 24). Top 10 social sites for finding a job. [Web blog post]. Retrieved from http://mashable.com/2009/02/24/top-10-social-sites-for-finding-a-job/

Scott, D. (n.d.). 11 Examples of online marketing success. Retrieved from http://www.hubspot.com/Portals/53/docs/ebooks/11%20examples%20of%20online%20marketing%20success%20final.pdf

The Secretan Center. (n.d.). The spark, the flame, and the torch: Inspire self. Inspire others. Inspire the world. [Website]. Retrieved from http://secretan.com/torch/torch_quotes.php

Smith, L. (2008, October 2). Deloitte Film Festival taps YouTube potential. [Web blog post]. Retrieved from http://talkingic.typepad.com/foureightys_lee_smith_tal/2007/09/deloitte-film-f.html

Sterne, J. (2010). Social media metrics: How to measure and optimize your marketing investment. Hoboken, NJ: John Wiley & Sons.

Surowiecki, J. (2005). *The wisdom of crowds.* New York: Anchor Books.

Wladawsky-Berger, I. (2009, November 30). Social media implications for business. [Web blog post]. Retrieved from http://blog.irvingwb.com/blog/2009/11/social-media-implications-for-business-html